WORKING WORLD

Language and Culture of the Job Market

MARIA MANISCALCO BASKIN   LOIS WASSERMAN MORTON

Harcourt Brace & Company

Orlando   San Diego   New York
Toronto   London   Sydney   Tokyo

PHOTO CREDITS

H. Armstrong Roberts, 1, 99
HBJ Photo, 15, 43, 79, 115, 133, 151, 177, 219
John Oldenkamp/Cynthia Sabransky, 27, 207
AT&T Photo Service, 61, 193
Harry Rinehart, 163

Drawings on page 161 by Jeremiah Lighter

Requests for permission to make copies of any part of the work should be
mailed to: Permissions Department, Harcourt Brace & Company, 8th Floor,
Orlando, Florida 32887.

ISBN: 0-15-596710-X

Printed in the United States of America

To David
  —my light
Jonathan
  —my rare jewel
Calogera Gerardi Galluzzo
  —my roots

MARIA BASKIN

To my husband, Henry,
  and my grandparents,
  Yetta and Philip Goldstein
  and Fanny and Paul Wasserman,
  who bravely overcame linguistic and
  cultural barriers in a new land

LOIS MORTON

PREFACE

This book is dedicated to the non-native adult who is studying English in order to advance professionally. It teaches language competency and presents information necessary for getting, keeping, and advancing in a job—information currently in demand for native speakers but not generally available to the student of English as a second language. We focus on the ongoing adjustment to American employment practices and on the cultural misperceptions that many non-native job seekers experience.

When there are cultural differences, misperceptions often arise, although they are usually not recognized as such, either by the non-native job seeker or by the employer or potential employer. In searching for incidents that would illustrate cultural misperceptions, we used as sources counselors, social workers, immigrants with many years of residence in America, and specialists in cross-cultural communication, all of whom have an overview of the cultural patterns of both the native and the non-native, as well as an objective understanding of the issues.

Each chapter is organized as follows:

1. A situational passage illustrating a cultural misperception serves to stimulate thought and discussion. This reading is followed by (a) comprehension questions, (b) inference questions, (c) vocabulary exercises, (d) a grammar review, and (e) idiom practice.

2. An informational passage containing practical cultural information about the working world helps the reader understand the cultural misperception illustrated in the situational passage. This second passage also contains tips or

guidelines to follow in unfamiliar situations. The reading is followed by (a) comprehension questions, (b) discussion, and (c) creative applications, in the form of dialogues, group-oriented tasks, and applied practice.

Most cultural misperceptions occur because of lack of information about cultural practices. This kind of information is not taught in the classroom but is understood by natives as "the way things are done." These unwritten rules are not obvious to the nonnative person, who must learn them through trial and error, often at the cost of confusion, resentment, distress, and embarrassment. It is our hope that this book provides information that will facilitate the non-native's adjustment to the working world.

Acknowledgments

We would like to acknowledge the following organizations for their contributions to this book: Federation Employment and Guidance Service, the Jewish Vocational Service of East Orange, and English in Action. Our thanks to all the counselors whose work with the emigre population has given them special sensitivity to cultural adjustment and who shared insights and case histories to help illustrate cultural misperceptions in the job search and on the job: Finola Bourke, Hannah Reich, Paula Trushin, Cynthia Martin, and Mary Mackler; and to the following emigres who shared with us the difficulties of their own adjustments: Lisa Raskin, Arkady Lirstman, and Constantin David.

Very special thanks are due to the former American Council for Emigres in the Profession, under the leadership of Lenore Parker, whose goals and services led to the formulation of the original concepts on which the book is based. We also wish to thank posthumously Elaine Newman of the Queens College English as a Second Language Program for allowing us the freedom to develop these materials in an academic setting.

We particularly wish to thank our editors, Nina Gunzenhauser, who originally believed in and commissioned the project, Marilyn Rosenthal and Jacqueline Flamm, who helped bring the manuscript to its present form, Cella Irvine, our copy editor, and Harry Rinehart, our patient and enthusiastic designer. We also wish to thank Virginia Martino for her valuable help with the glossary.

On a personal note: Maria Baskin wishes to thank her parents, Vita and Alberto Maniscalco, who gave her a life of rich experiences both in this country and abroad, and a special thanks to her husband, David Baskin, for being her muse and inspiring her to reach for more; Lois Morton wishes to thank her husband, Henry, for his love and guidance, her children, Philip and Amy, and her mother, Betty Goldstein Wasserman, for setting an inspiring example for her to follow.

CONTENTS

WORKING WORLD

Language and Culture of the Job Market

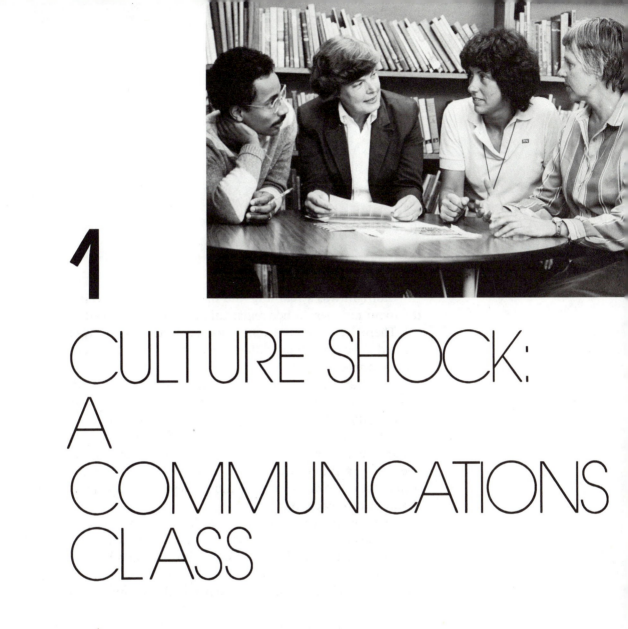

1
CULTURE SHOCK: A COMMUNICATIONS CLASS

Sunlight was streaming into the room. Lee looked in, checked the room number on her registration card, and walked in.

There were about twenty people seated in the room. They seemed to be from many different countries, but they were all here for one purpose.

A young woman entered the room. She smiled at the group and said, "Good morning!" They responded hesitantly with various greetings. Then the young woman asked the group to arrange their chairs in a circle. Many of the people were surprised at this request. As they began to stand up and move their chairs around, Lee recognized another member of the group, a woman she had seen in the office during registration. They smiled and pushed their chairs next to each other.

The young woman at the front of the room took a chair and joined the circle. "Let's begin by introducing ourselves," she said. "My name is Jane Walsh. I'm from California, and I teach English at this college. I will be your instructor for this Communications Skills class. Now, would you each tell the group a little about yourself?"

After the introductions were completed, Jane asked, "Why are you taking this Communications Skills course? Yes, Lee?"

Lee said, "I work as a bookkeeper, and I need to improve my English."

"Yes, Joseph?"

"I also want to improve my English, in order to get a better job." Joseph paused. "In my country I was a teacher of history . . . but not any more."

Victoria said, "I work with many Americans, and I have a difficult time understanding them over the telephone." Several people nodded.

"I am not working at the moment," Gisela said. "I'd like to begin to look for a job, but I don't know where or how to begin. It seems so difficult here."

"There are so many adjustments to make when you come to a new country," Jane said. "Language is only one of them. I would like you to think back to the time before you arrived in this country. When you were preparing to come to the United States, what did you think it would be like?"

Marisa looked confused. "Do you mean, how did we think it would be?" Jane nodded, and Marisa continued, "Well, that's easy. I pictured money all over the streets." Everyone laughed with her.

"You mean, the streets were 'paved with gold,'" said Victor.

"Of course, that's what I had always heard," commented Victoria. "And you, Peter, how did you picture things in the United States?"

Peter frowned before answering, "I thought it was easy to find any kind of job."

"Me, too," Martha called out. "I always heard America was the land of opportunity."

Jane then turned to Simon, who was sitting very quietly, and asked, "What about you?"

Simon smiled and said, "I had expected to have a job and an apartment waiting for me. I didn't expect to be completely on my own. In the country I came from they told you what to do. I never realized there would be so many decisions to make."

"Also," added Lee, "it was strange for me to come to a culture where people can disagree with the government. This freedom is difficult to get accustomed to."

"You didn't find what you had expected," said Jane. "Then, what did you find?"

Marisa spoke first. "I certainly didn't find any money in the streets. And I found jobs hard to get. I finally found a temporary job after I went to about ten different places."

"It's not the land of opportunity for me, either." said Simon. "I have been trying to get a job as an engineer for months. But I just don't understand how things work here."

"Well, Simon," said Jane, "in this communications class we're going to learn how things work here. During the time we spend together, we will talk about settling in the United States. We will discuss where we want to go professionally, and, most important, how we can get there."

What Happened?

In the blank space, write T *if the sentence is true,* F *if it is false.*

_____ 1. Jane Walsh comes from Canada.

_____ 2. Getting used to a new language is the only adjustment you make when you come to a new country.

_____ 3. For Simon, it was difficult to get used to making so many decisions.

_____ 4. Several people found it hard to understand English over the telephone.

_____ 5. Several people in the class said that jobs were hard to get.

_____ 6. Joseph is a history teacher now.

Hidden Meanings

Think about the following questions carefully before discussing in class. If necessary, refer to the story.

1. Why did Simon expect to have a job waiting for him?

2. Why do you think that moving their chairs into a circle was surprising to the class?

3. What did Simon mean when he said, "I don't understand how things work here?"

4. Why did Lee feel that freedom was difficult to get accustomed to?

5. When Jane said that "language is only one of the adjustments a person has to make in a new country," what did she mean?

6. Why did everyone think America was such a rich country?

4

Circle the letter of the expression that has the same meaning as the underlined word or words.

1. They responded <u>hesitantly</u> with various greetings.
   a. confidently
   b. uncertainly
   c. quickly

2. She <u>pictured</u> money in the streets.
   a. illustrated
   b. saw in her mind
   c. hoped for

3. Marisa looked <u>confused</u> by the question.
   a. angry
   b. embarrassed
   c. puzzled

4. The streets were <u>paved</u> with gold.
   a. covered
   b. colored
   c. on top of

5. "Of course, that's what I always heard," <u>commented</u> Victoria.
   a. called out
   b. said
   c. interrupted

Complete each statement using one of the vocabulary words underlined in the text.

1. To show concentration or displeasure with a facial expression is

   to _____ .

2. To express a different opinion from another person is to

   _____ .

3. To move your head up and down is to

   _____ .

4. To see someone or something that looks familiar is to

_____ it.

5. To get used to something new is to become

_____ to it.

Understanding Words

Which statement is a good example of the meaning of the vocabulary word? Circle A or B.

1. hesitantly
   A. "Excuse me . . . but . . . could you tell me . . . "
   B. "All right, all right, I'm the manager. What is the problem here?"

2. realize
   A. "Now I understand why you couldn't call me. Your car broke down on the highway."
   B. "I fail to understand why Peter isn't here, and why he has not called me."

3. disagree
   A. "What you say is true."
   B. "I have a completely different opinion."

4. expect
   A. "I think about fifty people will come to our Christmas party."
   B. "I put an ad in the paper to sell my car, and I have no idea how many people will call."

5. request
   A. "May I have a container of milk, please?"
   B. "Is Maria absent today?"

6. confused
   A. "Which road did he tell us to take? I thought he said Exit 38, but there are two signs here, 38 North and 38 South."
   B. "I'm really embarrassed about all these words I spelled wrong. I'll check more carefully in the future."

Look at these question forms.

	Jane	speaks	several languages
Does	Jane	speak	several languages?
	They	speak	English.
Do	they	speak	English?
	She	spoke	to the students.
Did	she	speak	to the students?
	He	asked	a question.
Did	he	ask	a question?

Change the following statements to questions.

Example: a. He *practices* English every evening.
       Does he *practice* English every evening?

       b. Jane *began* the lesson.
       Did Jane *begin* the lesson?

1. She *asked* everyone to sit in an open circle.

   _____

2. She *pulled* up a chair and joined them.

   _____

3. Joseph *wants* to get a better job.

   _____

4. He *taught* history.

   _____

5. Victoria *works* with many Americans.

   _____

6. All newcomers *go through* some kind of adjustment period when they enter a new culture.

   _____

7. She *spoke* to each person in a friendly way.

_____

8. Lee *feels* that she needs to improve her English.

_____

9. They *pushed* their chairs next to each other.

_____

Say It This Way

From the list below choose an idiom that has the same meaning as the underlined phrase, and rewrite the complete sentence.

to pull up
how things work
to be hard to get
to be on one's own
the streets are paved with gold

1. In the current employment market jobs are <u>difficult to obtain</u>.

_____

_____

2. In a new culture it takes time to learn <u>what the procedures are</u>.

_____

_____

3. Some newcomers think <u>it's easy to make money</u> in the United States.

_____

_____

4. "Michael, <u>bring</u> a chair and join the discussion."

_____

_____

5. "When I arrived in the United States, I found an apartment, I found a job, and I was totally <u>independent</u>."

_____

_____

The process of adjusting to life in a new country is often called "culture shock." The word *culture* as used here has a different meaning than it usually does. Frequently, the word *culture* pertains to music, literature, art, and higher education. Here, though, *culture* means the customs of a society and the way in which people **interact** with each other.

Every culture has certain basic ideas on which it is *built* and which everyone accepts as true. These are fundamental things that everyone "knows" which are learned in childhood, and which are automatic to the people who live in that culture. They include everything from the common **courtesies** and details of daily life to the deeper issues of a person's place in society, of family, of life and death, and even of the **attitude** towards time and space.

When a person enters a new culture, the basic customs and ideas that he or she automatically accepted may no longer be true. There is a new set of customs and attitudes to learn about and try to understand. During this period of adjustment a person feels a great **range** of emotions, from happiness and **excitement** to **loneliness**, anger, **discouragement**, and **depression**. This period of "culture shock" has been described as having approximately seven **stages**. On a simple line **graph** it appears like this:

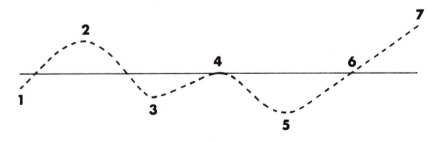

Courtesy of English in Action, New York, NY.

Stage 1: Some **anxiety** about leaving to go to a new country. What will I find there?

Stage 2: Excitement. Everything is new and interesting. I feel a little like a tourist.

Stage 3: Unhappiness as I realize that things are very different in the new culture. I miss friends and family, and I am lonely.

Stage 4: **Superficial** adjustment in establishing day-to-day **routines**. I feel satisfaction and a sense of **overcoming** problems.

Stage 5: Discouragement and **loss** of **self-esteem**. It is not so easy, after all, to know how things are done. The language is more difficult than I originally thought. I am an **outsider**; I am treated like a child; the natives are unfriendly. I cannot understand people and that makes me feel uncomfortable and angry. I am not what I was before, and my own culture has no meaning in this new country.

Stage 6: Growing understanding of the language and customs. My **self-confidence** and sense of **humor** are beginning to return. I am forming friendships in my new culture. I am beginning to see that all the problems in the new culture are not for **foreigners** alone, but that natives also experience some of them.

Stage 7: Feelings of acceptance—both accepting and being accepted by the native population. A psychological bridge is growing between the present and the past. I am both the person I was in my old culture and the person I am now in my new culture.

Some people need more time to adjust than other people, and some find it more difficult to adjust than others. But everyone entering a new culture experiences culture shock to some degree.

What seems to be common to all newcomers is the basic human need to understand and to be understood.

Glossed Words

(to) **interact**	(to) communicate verbally or nonverbally with others
courtesies	polite behavior
attitude	opinion about something
range	distance from one point to another
excitement	strong feelings of interest and emotion
loneliness	isolation; feelings of being alone without companions
discouragement	hopelessness
depression	low spirits or vitality; sadness
stage	phase
line graph	a chart that indicates any sort of relationship between two or more things
anxiety	feelings of nervousness
superficial	not real or genuine
routines	habits
overcoming	succeeding; conquering
loss	something that cannot be found
self-esteem	good opinion of oneself
outsider	one who is outside the culture
self-confidence	trust and belief in one's abilities
sense of humor	ability to appreciate and express what is funny
foreigners	citizens or natives of another country

What's It All About?

Answer the following questions with your teacher or in writing on a separate sheet of paper.

1. What are the phases of adjustment to a new culture?

2. What happens to a person entering a new culture?

3. What are some of the fundamental ideas that exist in every culture and that everyone accepts as true?

4. What are some of the emotions a person experiences while adjusting to a new culture?

Can We Talk?

Discuss the following questions with a partner, in small groups, or in a large group with your teacher.

1. What do you think of these phases of adjustment, and can you identify with any of them?

2. What advice would you give to someone who was entering the United States to live?

Putting It to Work

Use the following guided composition to discuss your own experience.

I have been in the United States ＿＿＿＿＿＿＿＿＿＿＿＿＿.

Before I came to this country I thought it would be ＿＿＿＿＿

＿＿＿＿＿＿＿＿＿＿＿＿＿＿＿＿＿＿＿＿＿＿.

I always heard ＿＿＿＿＿＿＿＿＿＿＿＿＿＿＿＿＿＿＿＿

about this country.

When I arrived I ＿＿＿＿＿＿＿＿＿＿＿＿＿＿＿＿＿.

I felt ＿＿＿＿＿＿＿＿＿＿＿＿＿＿＿＿＿＿.

My relatives ＿＿＿＿＿＿＿＿＿＿＿＿＿＿＿＿＿.

I had to make many new decisions. I had to _____

_____

_____ .

I found a job after _____ .

The most difficult thing for me was _____

_____ .

Now I feel I _____

_____ .

In this course I want to learn how to _____

_____ .

I want to learn these things so that in the future I can _____

_____ .

2
TIME:
VICTOR'S STORY

"In America, they live by the appointment book," Andre told his friend Victor. "When you walk into an office, the first question they ask you is, 'Do you have an appointment?' If you say no they tell you, 'I'm sorry, Mr. So & So can't see anyone without an appointment.'"

Victor had recently arrived in the United States, and he did not completely understand the need for appointments. He thought his friend was exaggerating. "If I go there and wait," Victor thought, "won't they have to see me?"

One day he went to an employment agency. This agency specialized in placing people with his qualifications. Victor wanted to start working as soon as possible so he could afford his own apartment. He was living with his brother and sister-in-law and he felt that he was imposing on them because they had a large family and a small house.

When he arrived at the agency at 10 A.M., the receptionist said to him, "Do you have an appointment?" Victor looked around the office and said, "No, I don't, but I see that there are very few people waiting here. I'm sure the counselor can see me." The receptionist answered, "I'm sorry. This agency works by appointment only." She told him to leave his résumé, fill out an application, and make an appointment. Victor did not have a résumé, but he was able to get an appointment in two days.

After he walked out, he thought of the long trip back home. Had he traveled all the way to the agency for nothing? Victor felt frustrated. He went back to the agency and explained to the receptionist that it was important for him to see the placement counselor today. He told her that he was prepared to wait until six o'clock if necessary in order to see her.

The receptionist sounded like a broken record. She continued to repeat, "This agency works by appointment only, by appointment only . . ." Victor realized that he needed to talk to someone who could give him more information.

Before dinner that evening, Victor <u>dropped in</u> on his friend Andre. He told him again why sometimes in America you cannot just drop in. Victor then turned to his friend and said, "Andre, you are right. In America you don't live from day to day—you live from appointment to appointment!"

What Happened?

Circle the letter of the word or words that best complete the statement.

1. When you walk into an office the receptionist asks,
   a. "What time is it?"
   b. "Do you have your appointment book?"
   c. "Do you have an appointment?"

2. Victor went to an employment agency that
   a. someone told him about.
   b. was not very good.
   c. specialized in his field.

3. When Victor walked into the employment agency he saw
   a. an office full of people.
   b. only the receptionist.
   c. not many people.

4. The receptionist suggested that Victor
   a. talk to someone immediately.
   b. wait for the manager.
   c. make an appointment with a counselor.

5. The receptionist sounded like
   a. a phonograph.
   b. a stereo.
   c. a broken record.

Hidden
Meanings

Think about the following questions carefully before discussing in class. If necessary, refer to the story.

1. What did Andre mean when he said, "Americans live by the appointment book"?

2. Why did Victor think Andre was exaggerating?

3. How would you explain why the placement counselor couldn't see Victor even though the office was empty?

4. Why did Victor feel that he needed more information?

Finding
the Definition

Circle the letter of the expression that has the same meaning as the underlined word or words.

1. He thought his friend was <u>exaggerating</u>.
   a. telling the truth
   b. shouting to make his point understood
   c. making something seem more or less than it was

2. One day he went to an <u>employment agency</u>.
   a. unemployment office
   b. new job
   c. organization that finds jobs

3. The employment agency <u>places</u> people.
   a. helps people to find jobs
   b. interviews
   c. finds them a place to live

4. This agency specialized in placing people with his <u>qualifications</u>.
   a. nationality
   b. education and work experience
   c. personality

5. When Victor had to go home without seeing a counselor, he felt <u>frustrated</u>.
   a. powerful and angry

b. happy and resigned
  c. angry and helpless

6. He wanted a job so he could <u>afford</u> his own apartment.
  a. move out of
  b. have enough money for
  c. live in

Complete each statement using one of the vocabulary words underlined in the text.

1. A special book you use to write appointments in is an

  _____ _____ .

2. To concentrate in one area of study or work is to

  _____ .

3. To make things difficult, or take advantage of someone is to

  _____ .

4. A person who gives advice is a _____ .

5. A person employed to receive callers and answer the telephone

  is a _____ .

6. A written summary of your education and work experience is

  your _____ .

Which statement is a good example of the meaning of the vocabulary word? Circle A or B.

1. <u>qualifications</u>
  A. "I'm a very active person, I enjoy reading, and next semester I will take a course at New York University."
  B. "I have ten years of experience as a secretary, and I have thirty college credits in secretarial studies."

2. to impose
   A. "I know you're tired, and I know it's very late, but I just have so much more to tell you; let's keep talking."
   B. "I'm glad you wanted to meet me for lunch, because I love talking to you."

3. frustrated
   A. "I'm going to call my counselor tomorrow morning and discuss my résumé."
   B. "I'm never going to an agency again. It's no use—I'll never get a job! I feel like a failure."

4. exaggerate
   A. "I just started a new job as a bookkeeper. They like me so much, they will probably give me a $5,000 raise next month."
   B. "I just started a new job as a bookkeeper. The manager told me that I will get a $1,000 increase in salary each year."

5. to drop in
   A. "I have an appointment to see Miss Harris at 10:15."
   B. "Hello. I was just passing by your agency, and I decided to come in and talk to one of your counselors."

Learning through Practice: Prepositions of Time

Look at the following examples.

at expresses *a specific time of day or night*
   The meeting will begin at 11:15.
   I can give you an appointment at three o'clock.

in is used with *parts of the day*, with *months* when the month is used without a specific date, with *seasons*, and with *years*
   He reads the newspaper in the evening.
   His job will begin in April.
   She came here in 1978.
   They like to go to the beach in the summer.

in is sometimes used with *a future time*
   The wedding will be in three months.

on is used with *days of the week* and with *dates* that have numbers

I have an appointment with him on Wednesday.
She came here on October 1, 1978.

before means *earlier than*
Before I came to this country, I lived in Russia.

after means *later than*
November comes after October.

until means *up to the time of*
They talked until eight o'clock.
She stayed in the office until she finished her work.

Underline the correct one of the two prepositions in parentheses.

1. He arrived there (at, on) 10 A.M.

2. I came to this country (in, on) September 10, 1977.

3. He decided to wait (before, until) six o'clock to see the counselor.

4. My birthday is (in, on) December.

5. She arrived at the meeting (before, until) me.

6. I will see you (after, in) ten minutes.

7. It's necessary to make an appointment (before, after) the job interview.

8. Mr. Jones comes to the office only (in, on) Wednesdays.

Say It This Way

Match the idioms in Column A with the definitions in Column B.

Column A	Column B
a. by the appointment book	＿＿ according to schedule
b. to sound like a broken record	＿＿ any last name
c. to drop in	＿＿ to repeat something over and over
d. to make an appointment	＿＿ to visit without an appointment
e. Mr. So and So	＿＿ to get an appointment

Getting the Facts: The Use of Time in the Business World

Americans see time as an expensive object or material. We talk about time in many different ways. We save it, earn it, waste it, spend it, kill it! Time is money. We **invest** it, we carefully **budget** it. We have free time, **leisure** time, **spare** time. We are paid time-and-a-half for working overtime. We place more stress on time than almost any other culture in the world.

American business organizations are especially interested in the **efficient** use of time. In the business world, you almost always need appointments for interviews, meetings, and luncheons. An American businessman or businesswoman may even make an appointment for a phone call.

One business organization that you may use when you are job-hunting is an employment agency. Some employment agencies see applicants without an appointment. These include the state employment services and **nonprofit** agencies that do not receive fees for finding jobs for people. There are also some private employment agencies that do not require appointments, even though they do receive a fee. These are usually the agencies that deal with secretarial and **nonskilled** positions. Counselors there may spend only a few minutes with each applicant.

But an agency that deals with technical and higher-salaried jobs, spends much more time with each applicant. Appointments are necessary in this type of agency, where a counselor may be able to see only a few applicants a day.

An interview for any kind of job, whether the interview is obtained through a friend, a classified **advertisement**, or an agency, generally requires an appointment. It is important to be on time for your appointment. If you have made an appointment and cannot keep it, or if you will be more than ten minutes late, you should always call the interviewer. If you do not cancel the appointment or **notify** the interviewer that you will be late, you will create a negative impression on your possible employer.

To make efficient use of time, American business people schedule their days hour by hour. In most American business situations, appointments are a necessary courtesy.

(to) **invest** time	(to) spend time in order to increase future profit
(to) **budget** time	(to) plan for future use of time
leisure time	free or unoccupied time
spare time	free or extra time
efficient	economical or proper use
nonprofit	not for earning money
nonskilled	having no trade
classified advertisement	newspaper listing of jobs
(to) **notify**	(to) inform

What's It All About?

Answer the following questions with your teacher or in writing on a separate sheet of paper.

1. How do Americans view time?

2. At what kinds of employment agencies are appointments necessary?

3. If you cannot keep an appointment, what should you do?

4. If you don't call when you cannot keep an appointment for a job, what may happen?

Can We Talk?

Discuss the following questions with a partner, in a small group, or in a large group with your teacher.

1. In your country, is it necessary to make appointments? When is it necessary? When isn't it necessary?

2. In your country, is it the custom to drop in on friends without calling? In America, how do people feel about dropping in? When can you drop in? When can't you drop in?

Putting It to Work: Making and Breaking Interviews

In Exercises I and II, first read the conversation with a partner; then, with your partner, use the guide to make up your own conversation.

I. *Read the following conversation with a partner.*

A: Good morning, Grayson Consultants.

B: Hello. My name is _____ . I would like some information about your agency. Perhaps you can help me.

A: I'll try. What would you like to know?

B: Does your agency work by appointment only or can I drop in any time during the week?

A: Our agency works by appointment. We place applicants in high-level positions. Would you like to make an appointment to see an employment counselor at our agency?

B: Yes I would, thank you.

A: What type of position are you looking for?

B: I have a degree in chemical engineering and I have five years of experience in the field.

A: Fine. Can you come on Monday at 11:15 A.M.?

B: Yes, that's perfect. I will be there. And what is your name, please.

A: My name is _____ .

B: OK, then, _____ , I will see you on Monday at 11:15 A.M. Thank you and have a good day.

A: You too. Goodbye.

Working in pairs, use the following guide to make an appointment.

Receptionist	Caller
1. Say greeting	
	2. Say greeting
	3. Ask for information about the agency

4. Give information and ask what caller is interested in

5. Give information about qualifications and interest

6. Set up appointment with counselor

7. Repeat and confirm appointment information

8. Close the conversation

9. Close the conversation

II. *Read the following conversation with a partner.*

A: Ace Employment Agency.
B: Hello, may I speak to _____ , please?
A: Who's calling, please?
B: This is _____ _____ .
A: One moment, please.
C: Hello?
B: Hello, _____ . This is _____ .
I'm very sorry, but I cannot keep my appointment with you today.
C: What's wrong?
B: I'm not feeling well.

or

Something came up and I can't make it.

or

My (wife, son, daughter . . .) is sick. I would like to make an appointment for next week.

C: All right. How about next Thursday at three?

B: Thursday at three? That's fine. Thank you very much.
C: You're welcome. See you then.

or

B: That's not a good time for me. How about four o'clock on Thursday?

C: That's fine. See you then. Have a good week.

B: Thank you. You too. Goodbye.

Working in pairs, use the following guide to break an appointment.

Receptionist	Caller
1. Say greeting	
	2. Say greeting
	3. Tell why you are calling, give specific reason, and ask for new appointment
4. Suggest new time	
	5. Accept new appointment and repeat appointment information
	or
	Reject the appointment and suggest another one
6. Confirm new appointment	
	7. Close the conversation
8. Close the conversation	

3

CHANGING JOBS: MARTHA'S STORY

Martha had been working for Miller Laboratories for two years, but she was not happy there. Nothing significant had happened in the way of promotions or salary increases. Martha felt that her supervisor, a younger and less experienced person than she, did not like her. In fact, the supervisor often said unpleasant things to her.

One day, while talking with her friend Maria, she mentioned how discouraged she was. Maria gave her the name of a cousin of hers who was director of personnel for a large chemical company. He would at least be able to give her information on how one advances in the field of chemical research. She called him the next day and set up an interview on her lunch hour. He sounded so positive! It was the first good thing she had heard in a long time.

Martha's heart was beating quickly as she stepped out of the elevator on the tenth floor. "I have an appointment to see Mr. Petri," she told the receptionist.

"Just have a seat and his secretary will be with you shortly," said the receptionist, smiling.

While she was waiting, Martha glanced through some brochures about the company. Soon a young woman came out to the reception area. "Miss Alberta?" she asked. "Mr. Petri will see you now. Please follow me."

Martha entered the office of the director of personnel and sat down. The interview went well, and she knew she was making a good impression. Mr. Petri was impressed with her education and experience, and he complimented her on her English.

"You're just the kind of person we need here," he said. "You're being wasted in your other job. Let me see what we can do for you.

Give me a call in a day or two. I'm sure we can find a place for you in our organization."

Martha was so happy she almost danced out of the building. She thought, "In just a few days I will change to a better job. What good luck that I spoke to Maria about my problem."

That afternoon, Ruth Kenny, her supervisor, was particularly irritating. She saw that Martha had come in ten minutes late from her lunch hour and she said very sarcastically, "Oh, so you finally decided to come back to work today?"

This was the last straw. She could not take another insult. Besides, Mr. Petri was right; she was being wasted in this job.

"Look," she said angrily, "if you don't like the way I work, I don't need to stay here. I can get a better job. I'll go where I'm appreciated! Good-bye!" She grabbed her things and stormed out of the office.

Martha was excited by the day's events. That night she called Maria and told her what had happened. When Martha finished her whole story, she asked Maria, "What do you think?"

Maria didn't answer immediately. Then she said cautiously, "Do you really want my opinion?"

"Of course!"

"Well," said Maria carefully, "are you sure about the other job?"

"Well, not exactly, but . . ."

Maria continued, "Will you be able to get a recommendation from Ms. Kenny if you need one?"

"A recommendation? . . . from Ms. Kenny?" hesitated Martha, in a worried tone.

"And didn't you have to give notice?"

"Give notice?" asked Martha nervously.

"Martha, I hope you didn't burn your bridges," Maria said. "I think I would have handled it differently."

What Happened?

Circle the letter of the word or words that best complete the statement.

1. Martha is unhappy in her job because
   a. she has not advanced.
   b. her supervisor is younger than she is.
   c. the work is not significant.

2. Martha got the name of a director of personnel through
   a. her cousin.
   b. her friend.
   c. an agency.

3. Mr. Petri
   a. offered Martha a job.
   b. didn't like Martha.
   c. felt Martha was not valued in her present job.

4. Martha's interview with the Personnel Director was
   a. at the end of the day.
   b. during working hours.
   c. on her lunch hour.

5. Martha was so angry at her supervisor that she
   a. quit her job.
   b. gave a week's notice.
   c. controlled her temper.

Hidden Meanings

Think about the following questions carefully before discussing in class. If necessary, refer to the story.

1. What did Mr. Petri mean when he said, "I'm sure we can find a place for you in our organization"?

2. Why did Martha dance out of the office after her job interview?

3. Why did she lose her temper?

4. Why did Martha's friend speak cautiously on the telephone?

Finding the Definitions

Circle the letter of the expression that has the same meaning as the underlined word or words.

1. She grabbed her things angrily.
   a. threw down
   b. hit
   c. took quickly

2. The supervisor was <u>particularly irritating</u> when she said, "So, you decided to come back to work today."
   a. especially angry
   b. especially nice
   c. especially annoying

3. You are very skilled; your talents are <u>wasted</u> in this job.
   a. not good enough
   b. not fully used
   c. useful

4. Martha was <u>discouraged</u> about improving her position at Miller Laboratories.
   a. enthusiastic
   b. confused
   c. without hope

5. She <u>stormed</u> out of the office and slammed the door.
   a. ran
   b. rushed angrily
   c. tiptoed

Finding the Word

Complete each statement using one of the vocabulary words underlined in the text.

1. A raise in salary is an _____ .

2. To look quickly is to _____ .

3. To inform the employer in advance that you are leaving the job

   is to _____ .

4. Receiving a higher position in your place of work is getting a

   _____ .

5. To lose hope is to feel _____ .

6. Scholarly or scientific investigation is called _____ .

7. A booklet or pamphlet containing particular information is a

   _____ .

Understanding Words

Which statement is a good example of the meaning of the vocabulary word? Circle A or B.

1. sarcastic
   A. "You only took fifteen minutes for lunch. Why don't you leave a little early today?"
   B. "You're late—did you go to China for lunch today?"

2. appreciate
   A. "Your work is really excellent. I'm very happy that I hired you."
   B. "You finished the report on time, but there are a few things I don't like."

3. give notice
   A. "I will be leaving in two weeks."
   B. "I'm leaving today. I've found another job."

4. discouraged
   A. "I have looked and looked for a new job, but I'm beginning to think I won't find one."
   B. "I have been looking for a new job for months, but I'm sure I will find one soon."

5. cautious
   A. "I sometimes cross the street when the light is red.
   B. "I always look several times in both directions before crossing the street."

6. compliment
   A. "I love the color blue."
   B. "That's a lovely suit you're wearing . . . I love the color."

Learning through Practice: Direct and Indirect Speech

Look at the following two sentences.

1. Martha said, "I have an appointment to see Mr. Greene."
2. Martha said that she had an appointment to see Mr. Greene.

The first sentence is an example of *direct speech* because the words of the speaker are in quotation marks and are shown exactly as she spoke them. The second sentence is an example of *indirect* speech because the words of the speaker are reported indirectly.

When indirectly reporting what another person said, you must often change the pronouns, adverbs, and verb tenses. Study the examples below before you do the exercise.

Direct Speech	*Indirect Speech*
He said, "It's snowing hard."	He said (that) it was snowing hard.
"The office usually closes early during a snowstorm."	the office usually closed early during a snowstorm.
"I'm going home."	he was going home.
"She went home."	she had gone home.
"They've told everyone to leave early."	they had told everyone to leave early.
"We will go home."	they (or we) would go home.
"You can go home."	I (or we) could go home.
"You should go home."	I (or we) should go home.
"The storm may get worse."	the storm might get worse.

Change each sentence from direct to indirect speech.

Example: Mr. Greene said, "I'm sure we can find a place for you here."

Mr. Greene said that he was sure they could find a place for me there.

_____

1. Yesterday the head of my department said, "I want to have a talk with you."

_____

_____

2. She said, "I am sorry to hear that you are looking for another job."

_____

_____

3. She said, "I hope I can convince you to stay."

_____

_____

4. My supervisor had told her, "I am impressed with how quickly Lee has learned his job."

_____

_____

5. I said, "I really like my work and all the people here."

_____

_____

6. But I said, "I don't feel that our organization offers an opportunity for me to advance."

_____

_____

7. She said, "It's true that there are no openings that would give you a promotion."

_____

_____

8. Then she said, "We may be expanding soon, and we will need another supervisor."

_____

_____

9. She said, "You should do what seems best for you."

_____

_____

10. I thanked her and said, "I will think about it."

_____

_____

Say It This Way

Match the idioms in Column A with the definitions in Column B.

Column A	Column B
a. the last straw	____ to inform your employer in advance that you are leaving the job
b. to have a seat	____ to give someone a good opinion of you
c. at least	____ telephone me
d. give me a call	____ to make it impossible to return
e. to set up	____ at the minimum, the smallest amount
f. to burn your bridges	____ can't accept it, can't tolerate it
g. to give notice	____ to look quickly through
h. to glance through	____ to sit down
i. "I can't take it"	____ the final unpleasant thing
j. to lose your temper	____ to arrange
k. to make a good impression	____ to be angry without control

Getting the Facts: Changing Jobs

Some people say that Americans go to work with **résumés** in their pockets. In this country, it is not unusual for people to change jobs **frequently**; changing jobs is a way of **advancing professionally** and **financially**. It is not considered strange for a person to have three or four jobs over a period of ten years.

If you have a job and want to change it, keep the old job while you look for a new one. Having a job gives you an **advantage**. You can take your time and be **selective**. You also have more **bargaining power**. You may get a better salary offer if a prospective employer knows you are not in urgent need of a job.

Here are some tips:

1. **Define** your present job and write down a **job description** of it.
2. List the **pros and cons** of staying with your present job.
3. Look through the **want ads** and see what is **available** to you based on your qualifications and experience.
4. If you have a résumé, bring it up to date. If not, write one. (We will be looking at résumés in Chapter 6.)
5. Let friends know that you want to change jobs.
6. Find out if there are professional organizations in your field. **Investigate** them in order to make new contacts and find out the current "buzz words" (special vocabulary in the field).
7. Go on as many interviews as you can, whether they are for general information, a *possible* job offer, or a *concrete* (definite) job offer for a position that is open. Even if the job is not exactly what you want, going on interviews is a way of keeping your name in **circulation**, and it is a learning experience for your next interview.
8. Don't do anything to **endanger** your present job. For example, go on job interviews before or after working hours or on lunch hours.
9. Be sure that you have a new job before you give notice at your old job.
10. Always give the employer enough notice to find a substitute for you. For most jobs this should be at least two weeks; it should never be less than one week.

11. Always leave on a positive note. You may need a **reference** from your former employer sometime in the future.

Changing jobs is difficult, but if you **approach** it with careful planning, it can bring good results.

Glossed Words

résumé	summary of one's employment record
frequently	often; repeatedly
advancing	going forward; being promoted
professionally	having to do with one's occupation or job
financially	having to do with money
advantage	anything favorable
selective	careful in one's choices
bargaining power	greater control when discussing terms, or negotiating
(to) **define**	(to) explain; specify exactly
job description	duties and responsibilities of a job
pros and cons	reasons for and against something
want ads	job advertisement section in newspaper
available	ready; usable; obtainable
(to) **investigate**	(to) examine; (to) look or inquire into
(to) keep in **circulation**	(to) keep in motion
(to) **endanger**	(to) put in danger
reference	recommendation
(to) **approach**	(to) come near something

What's It All About?

Answer the following questions with your teacher or in writing on a separate sheet of paper.

1. Why isn't it unusual for people in the U.S. to change jobs?

2. Why should you keep your old job while you look for a new one?

3. Why is it important to write down the pros and cons of staying on a job?

4. What are "buzz words"?

Can We Talk?

Discuss the following questions with a partner, in small groups, or in a large group with your teacher.

1. If you want time off from your present job to go for another interview, how would you ask your employer?

2. How do you know when an employer is making a serious job offer?

3. Should Martha have taken the job interview seriously? Why or why not?

4. Was Martha wise to answer her supervisor the way she did? How else could she have answered her?

Putting It to Work

Job Titles

accountant	carpenter	employment coun-
baby sitter	cashier	selor
baker	computer pro-	engineer
bank teller	grammer	file clerk
barber, hairstylist	construction	firefighter
bartender	worker	florist
bookkeeper	cook	furrier
building super-	custodian	gardener, land-
intendent	dental assistant	scaper
bus driver	doctor	housekeeper
butcher	electrician	house painter

interpreter   pharmacist   social worker
key punch   plumber   stock clerk
  operator   police officer   tailor
librarian   printer   taxi driver
live-in companion   railroad conductor   teacher
manager   receptionist   translator
mechanic   salesperson   travel agent
messenger   secretary   typist
nurse   security guard   waiter
nurse's aide   sewing machine
pattern maker   operator

1. Which of these jobs are not familiar to you?

2. What are some other jobs that could be added?

3. Form into small groups. Choose four of the above jobs and discuss the duties and responsibilities of these jobs. For each job you choose, ask yourself, "What does a _____ do?" and share your answers with the group. Select one person to write down the group's collective response.

Assignment: Finding "Buzz Words"

Look in the want ads, or telephone-book yellow pages, under the job headings listed in the column at the left, and find three buzz words that appear in the advertisements for each job title.

Secretary			
Computer programmer			
Bookkeeper			
Travel agent			
Laboratory technician			

Telephoning for Information

Sometimes during a job search you may want to call and ask for information about a company. You may need to find out someone's name, for example, or you may want to request an annual report, which is a summary of the company's yearly earnings and activities.

Practice the following dialogue with another student.

Receptionist:	Riverside Packing Company. Good morning.
Caller:	Hello, my name is _____. Am I speaking with the receptionist?
Receptionist:	Yes, you are. May I help you?
Caller:	I was hoping that you could. I am planning to send your personnel department my résumé. I was wondering if you would know the best person to send it to, and his or her title.
Receptionist:	Well, I don't think there are any positions open at the moment. What kind of job are you looking for?
Caller:	I am presently employed elsewhere. I have looked into your company, and am very impressed with it. That is why I need to know the best person to send my correspondence to. Can you help me?
Receptionist:	Well, I guess the best person would be Mr. Smith. He's the personnel manager.
Caller:	Smith, is that S-M-I-T-H? And his first name?
Receptionist:	Robert.
Caller:	And is there a room number or a floor that I should write down?
Receptionist:	Yes, fifth floor, room 539.
Caller:	And that's at 37 Porter Street, New Town, New Jersey?
Receptionist:	Yes, that's correct.
Caller:	Well, you have really been helpful. I appreciate your taking the time. Have a good day, and thanks again.
Receptionist:	You're welcome, and good luck.

Other phrases

"I am very interested in your company. Could you send me an annual report, please?"

"Could you tell me the name of your personnel manager, please?"

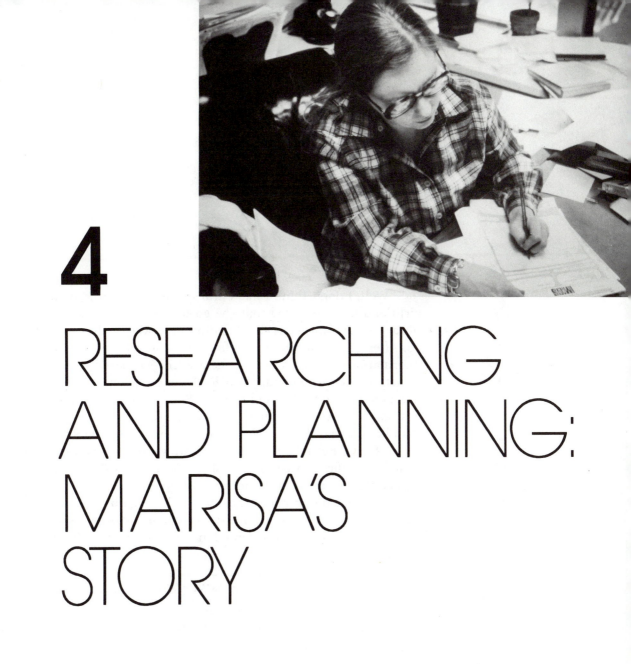

4

RESEARCHING AND PLANNING: MARISA'S STORY

"Well, I don't think I like Carol's idea," thought Marisa. Her girlfriend had <u>suggested</u> that she go to the <u>career</u> section of the library to get some ideas about finding a job. Marisa didn't want to go. After all, what would she find in the library? Books full of information. That wasn't what she needed. She needed a new job, something that would really <u>utilize</u> all her experience. The job she had now was so <u>boring</u> and <u>routine</u>. She wanted to move on to a position that would be more satisfying. After all, she had more than her clerical skills to offer an employer. Back in her country, she had taught elementary school for two years, she had also completed a <u>certificate</u> program in fashion design, and she had been a supervisor in a dress manufacturing company.

She decided that her best bet would be to go back to the <u>help wanted</u> ads. When she got home she sat down and began <u>skimming</u> the want ads. She circled several that looked <u>promising</u>, but one in particular caught her eye.

PRODUCTION ASSISTANT: FASHION

Bright, <u>knowledgeable</u> individual
to work in busy, exciting fashion
house. Must have good clerical
skills. Call 212 638-4382

Marisa decided to call immediately, and to her surprise she was connected very quickly. She spoke to the production manager, who made an appointment with her to come down to his office the next afternoon.

When she arrived, Mr. Swanson asked her for her résumé, briefly interviewed her, and then took her into a testing room where a personnel assistant gave her a very extensive battery of tests. Marisa was confident, because she knew she had done well.

When Marisa had completed the testing, she was escorted back to the production manager's office for a final interview.

"Well, Ms. Boca," began Mr. Swanson, "you certainly have done extremely well—in fact, too well—on the tests we gave you. And I must say, I'm not surprised, now that I've had time to study your résumé."

Marisa just looked at him in <u>bewilderment</u>. "I don't know what you mean," she replied.

"Please don't misunderstand me. You have excellent qualifications. But you have more than we need for this job. You have a college degree, and you've been a supervisor. This is an <u>entry-level</u> position. We feel that you would quickly realize this yourself and become <u>discontented</u>," continued Mr. Swanson.

"But this job is perfect for me," protested Marisa. "I have only been in this country for one year. I feel this is the right place for me to begin."

"It probably is, but your résumé automatically places you at a more advanced level and <u>eliminates</u> you from the assistant level." Mr. Swanson told Marisa that he would love to sit and talk with her, but he had other interviews.

"I can't believe it," thought Marisa, as she left the building. "I just can't believe it. Overqualified!" There had to be some way to present her experience on a résumé to fit the kind of job she wanted. Maybe she had better make a trip to the library after all, to learn how to get job-related information.

What Happened?

Write T *if the sentence is true,* F *if it is false.*

____ 1. Marisa wanted to get a new job in the career section of the library.

____ 2. She had been a teacher in her native country.

____ 3. She did not want an entry-level position.

_____ 4. On the day of her interview she went through an extensive battery of tests.

_____ 5. Mr. Swanson did not hire her because she was discontented.

_____ 6. She decided it would be a good idea to visit the library.

Hidden Meanings

Think about the following questions carefully before discussing in class. If necessary, refer to the story.

1. Why didn't Marisa want to go to the library at first?

2. Why did Marisa prefer an entry-level position to a higher position?

3. Why do you think an overqualified employee is a problem for an employer?

4. What did Mr. Swanson mean when he said that Marisa might quickly become discontented?

5. Why did Marisa change her mind about going to the library?

Finding the Definition

Circle the letter of the expression that has the same meaning as the underlined word.

1. Marisa looked at the manager in bewilderment.
   a. fear
   b. confusion
   c. delight

2. She had to complete a battery of tests.
   a. an electrical cell
   b. a series
   c. a page

3. One or two ads looked promising.
   a. hopeful

    b. certain

    c. useful

4. She wanted a job that would <u>utilize</u> her previous experience.
   a. give
   b. develop
   c. use

5. She began <u>skimming</u> the want ads.
   a. reading closely
   b. reading quickly
   c. cutting out

6. The job she had now was <u>boring</u> and <u>routine</u>.
   a. dull and automatic
   b. easy and satisfying
   c. interesting and low-paying

Finding the Word

Complete each statement using one of the vocabulary words under-lined in the text.

1. A job that you want to be your life's work is a _____ _____ .

2. To offer someone an idea for consideration is to _____ _____ it.

3. To remove or to take away something is to _____ _____ it.

4. A low-paying position at the beginning of a career is an _____ position.

5. A piece of paper that states you have successfully completed a course is a _____ .

6. The job listings in the classified section of the newspaper are also called _____ _____ ads.

Understanding Words

Which statement is a good example of the meaning of the vocabulary word? Circle A or B.

1. bewilderment
   A. "I'm trying to understand, but I have absolutely no idea what you are talking about."
   B. "I'm not sure what time the train arrives; let's check the timetable."

2. discontented
   A. "I'm not at all interested in ancient history."
   B. "I don't feel satisfied by my present job. I'd be happy to quit tomorrow."

3. knowledgeable
   A. "I've studied this problem for many years, and my experience tells me that we can't get results with our present method."
   B. "Of course, I'm just entering this business, and I have a great deal to learn."

4. suggest
   A. "Why don't you pay a visit to the local library?"
   B. "I enjoyed my visit to the public library."

Learning through Practice: Verb + Infinitive, Verb + Gerund

Some verbs take the infinitive form of another verb as their object. The most common of these are *want, need, hope, plan, decide, expect, intend, refuse,* and *like.* Look at the following sentences.

Verb + (want)	Infinitive (to go)
Marisa decided	to come to the United States.
She wants	to get a better job.
She hopes	to work in the fashion field.
She needs	to find out more information.
She plans	to go to the library.
She refuses	to remain in her present job.
She intends	to succeed.

```
    Verb        +           Infinitive
   (want)                    (to go)

She expects      to find a new job soon.
She would like   to become a fashion designer.
```

Interview a partner using the following questions. When you have finished, use the information to write a paragraph about your partner.

1. Why did you decide to come to the U.S.?

2. What do you want to do professionally?

3. What do you need to do this week?

4. What do you hope to do in the future?

5. What do you plan to do after this course?

6. How long do you intend to remain in this city?

7. What place would you most like to visit?

8. Is there something you refuse to do?

9. What do you expect a job interviewer to ask?

Other verbs in English take the gerund form of another verb as their object. The most common of these is *enjoy*. Look at the following sentences.

```
   Verb    +        Gerund (-ing)
  (enjoy)           (listening)

I enjoy     listening to music.
I enjoy     reading.
I enjoy     working with my hands.
I enjoy     running.
```

The verb *like* may take either the infinitive or the gerund. Look at the following sentences.

```
I like     to read.
I like     reading.
```

Interview a partner using the following questions. When you have finished, your partner will interview you.

1. Do you enjoy writing letters?

2. What other things do you enjoy doing?

3. Do you like reading mysteries?

4. What other things do you like doing?

5. Do you like to speak in front of people?

6. What other things do you like to do?

Say It This Way

Choose an idiom from the list below that has the same meaning as the underlined phrase, and rewrite the entire sentence.

(her) best bet
to catch one's eye
go through
to do well
I must say
to tailor (a résumé)
to look promising
to move on

1. She really <u>succeeded</u> in her business.

   _____

   _____

2. He had to <u>endure</u> a terrible period of adjustment.

   _____

   _____

3. This résumé is too general—you must <u>match</u> it to the job.

   _____

   _____

4. A very handsome man <u>attracted her attention</u>.

_____

_____

5. I've been in this job for five years—it's time <u>to go someplace else</u>.

_____

_____

6. Two of these ads look <u>like possibilities</u>.

_____

_____

7. The traffic is very heavy, so your <u>best course of action</u> is to take Route 27 instead of the expressway.

_____

_____

Getting the Facts: Research and Planning

Job-hunting in the United States is an active process. Americans are rushing to buy **best-selling** books that help the job seeker take control of the job search.

There are two essential steps in the job-hunting process: research and planning. Research means examining your skills and finding out where you can apply them. Planning means deciding how you will present your skills to a **prospective** employer. You should go through these steps carefully whether you are looking for your first job or you are interested in changing to a better job.

When examining your skills, ask yourself these questions:

What have I accomplished in my work experience?

What skills and personal **strengths** were necessary for those **accomplishments**?

What have I enjoyed doing most?

A Skills Inventory Form on pages 58–60 will help you to remember significant information.

When you understand what your strengths are, and what you have to offer an employer, you are ready to go to the career section of a library to identify some of your job possibilities. Here is a list of helpful **resources** that can be found in the library.

1. *Occupational Outlook Handbook.* Washington, D.C.: U.S. Government Printing Office, 1982.

> Reference book published by the federal government. Includes a guide to using the book, indexes, descriptions of occupations, and sources for more information. For each occupation there is a detailed description, including the type of the work, working conditions, training and other qualifications, earnings, related occupations and sources for more information.

2. *Dictionary of Occupational Titles.* Washington, D.C.: U.S. Government Printing Office, 1977.

> Two **volumes**; listing 35,000 job titles; describes what the job is, personality **traits** that fit the job, why and how the job is done, and provides good suggestions about **alternative** jobs and **cross-referencing**.

3. *Career and Occupational Literature.* New York: Federation Employment and Guidance Service, 1979.

> A **current reference**; provides information about 114 occupations, and resources where free literature is available upon request. Out of print, may be difficult to obtain in some libraries.

4. Teal, Everett A. *The Occupational Thesaurus.* Bethlehem, Pa.: Lehigh University, 1973.

> Two volumes; introduces college students to various fields and specific jobs in those fields; but good for everyone.

5. *Encyclopedia of **Associations**.* Detroit, Michigan: Gale Research Co., 1984. 5 volumes.

> Subtitle: A Guide to National and International Organizations. Provides information regarding organizations, including their size, goals, location.

6. Industrial and general business directories. These include the industrial classification and names of executives and provide a

guide to the size of the business by showing its financial **rating** and the number of employees.

    a. *MacRae's Industrial Directory. New York State. 1984.* New York: MacRae's Blue Book, Inc., 1984.

        Part of a series of directories of manufacturers for each state. Companies are listed by product, firm name, county and city, and SIC (Standard Industrial Classification) number.

    b. *Standard and Poor's Register of Corporations.* New York: Standard and Poor's, 1983. 3 vols.

        Vol. I lists corporations in the U.S., with names, titles, and functions of executive officers. Brief description of the business of each corporation. Over 40,000 corporations included. Vol. II is an alphabetical listing of individuals who head corporations. Vol. III consists of indexes. Supplements are published 3 times a year.

    c. *Thomas' Register of American Manufacturers.* New York: Thomas Publishing Co., 1984. 18 vols.

        Listing of products and services and manufacturers who provide same. Company profiles. Indexes.

    d. *Dun and Bradstreet—Million Dollar Directory.* Parsippany, N.J., 1983. 3. Vols.

        Lists approximately 115,000 U.S. businesses with a net worth of over $500,000. Alphabetically, geographically, by industry classification.

    e. *Standard Rate and Data.* Wilmette, Ill.: Standard Rate and Data Service. Published monthly.

        Professional publications in various fields, including newspapers and magazines.

Other Resources

1. Jackson, Tom and Davidyne Mayleas. *The Hidden Job Market for the 80s.* New York: Times Books, 1981.

    Includes information about alternatives to the "Help Wanted" section of the newspaper, e.g. networks, agencies, associations.

Emphasizes the importance of self-knowledge in finding the right job.

2. Lathrop, Richard. *Who's Hiring Who.* Berkeley, California: Ten Speed Press, 1977.

A guide to scouting the job market, writing a résumé, being interviewed.

3. Bolles, Richard Nelson. *What Color is Your Parachute?* Berkeley, California, 1984.

Popular, creative job hunting guide. Includes a list of resources.

Suggestions for Making a Job Change

1. Ask the librarian what books you can use for additional help in planning.
2. Find out the title of the directory of sources for your field.
3. Check through the *Occupational Thesaurus* and the *Dictionary of Occupational Titles* to see if you fit those descriptions of people well-suited to the type of job you want.
4. Find two publications in your field in *Standard Rate & Data.*
5. Find books and pamphlets to help you with résumé writing, interviewing, and so on.
6. List two professional associations in the field of your choice. It is valuable to make contacts through such associations.
7. List two companies in your field that you could approach for information or a job.
8. Send for an annual report of those companies. This will give you an indication of their financial position and their present and future interests.
9. List as many contacts as you can from these categories: family, friends, acquaintances, etc.
10. Get names of additional people you don't know from people you do know. This is called "networking." Try to ask people who would be in a position to help you find a job, or give you information about the field.

best-selling	popular
prospective	future
strengths	one's good abilities
accomplishments	successful completion of difficult tasks
resource	a source of information, such as a book or magazine.
volumes	books
traits	features; qualities
alternative	choice; another possibility
cross-referencing	directing from one part of a book to another part of the book
current	in progress; now
references	books, magazines, etc., that provide information.
associations	groups organized for a common purpose
rating	grade; evaluation

What's It All About?

Answer the following questions with your teacher or in writing on a separate sheet of paper.

1. Name one reference book in which you can find valuable information about all occupations.

2. What book will tell you sources of free literature about different occupations?

3. What reference book will tell you about professional associations?

4. What are two directories in which you can find corporations and businesses?

5. What is "networking"?

Can We Talk?

Discuss the following questions with a partner, in a small group, or in a large group with your teacher.

1. a. How would you define *skills, job responsibilities, personal strengths,* and *on-the-job accomplishments*?
   b. List some of your skills, job responsibilities, personal strengths, and on-the-job accomplishments.

2. How do your experiences while looking for a job compare with Marisa's?

3. a. Are you thinking of making a job change in the future?
   b. How can the library help you to research and plan your job search?

4. Is there a professional association for your occupation?

Putting It to Work: Skills Inventory Form

Look at the following examples of skills/responsibilities, personality traits, and accomplishments. Circle the ones that apply to you.

Skills/Responsibilities

verbs
(Use: I like _____ .)

acting	making crafts
analyzing	making decisions
assembling (putting things together)	meeting people
building things	negotiating (bargaining)
cooking	operating machines
dancing	organizing
decorating	persuading people
designing	repairing machines
driving	selling
filing	sewing
growing things	singing
helping people	solving problems
interviewing	speaking
listening	sports
	supervising

| teaching | working with numbers |
| typing | writing |

Personality Traits

adjectives	*nouns*
(Use: I am very	(Use: _____ is one of
_____.)	my strong points.)
accurate	accuracy
adaptable	adaptability
cooperative	cooperation
creative	creativity
dependable	dependability
flexible	flexibility
mature	maturity
organized	organization
persuasive	persuasiveness
punctual	punctuality
responsible	responsibility
tactful	tact

Accomplishments

I advanced to a higher position in ____ years.
I increased sales by ____ percent.
I designed a computer program.
I developed a new process for improving the quality of the work.
I improved the accounting system for my department by

_____.

Add some accomplishments of your own.

Whether you are currently looking for a job or will be looking sometime in the future, this form will help you organize your personal and professional experience. Read the following form and complete it with your personal, educational, and professional information.

SKILLS INVENTORY FORM

EDUCATION:

High School _____

Year graduated _____ Specialization _____

Trade School _____

Year graduated _____ Specialization _____

Certificate/diploma acquired _____

College _____

Year graduated _____ Specialization _____

Degree acquired _____

Other Education

School	Course	Skills

WORK EXPERIENCE: PART TIME or VOLUNTEER WORK

During High School years

Job title   *Skills acquired*
_____

_____

_____

_____

During college years

Company name   *Job Title*   *Skills acquired*
_____

_____

_____

_____

Other

Company name   *Job title*   *Skills acquired*
_____

_____

_____

_____

WORK EXPERIENCE: FULL TIME

Dates   *Company name*   *Job title*   *Responsibilities*   *Skills acquired*
_____

_____

_____

Looking over your work experience and the skills you have acquired, list your accomplishments at each job, regardless of how small or insignificant they may seem to you.

Name of company	Job title	Accomplishments

PERSONALITY TRAITS:

Trait	Application to work

HOBBIES: Things you have most enjoyed doing

_____

_____

_____

_____

5
TELEPHONING TO GET THE JOB: JOSEPH'S STORY

Receptionist:	Berkeley <u>Personnel</u>, good morning.
Joseph:	Yes, hello. I'm calling about the job you had in the paper. I would like to <u>arrange</u> for an interview.
Receptionist:	Which job are you inquiring about, and in which paper did you see it?
Joseph:	In last Sunday's *Herald Ledger*, and the job is for personnel <u>trainees</u>.
Receptionist:	May I have your name please?
Joseph:	Joseph Szeleskiewicz.
Receptionist:	Could you spell that please?
Joseph:	That's S-Z-E-L-E-S-K-I-E-W-I-C-Z.
Receptionist:	And that's pronounced "Seleskowitz"?

Joseph:	Yes.
Receptionist:	Hold on, please. I'll <u>switch</u> you to Mrs. Mitchell.
Mrs. Mitchell:	Hello, Mr. Szeleskiewicz? I understand you are interested in our personnel trainee positions?
Joseph:	Yes, I am.
	(*Pause*)
Mrs. Mitchell:	Could you tell me a little about your <u>background</u>, please.
Joseph:	Well, I have a degree in history, and I was a teacher in my country for five years. I've been in the United States for a year and a half, and I've been a taxi driver for the last eight months.
Mrs. Mitchell:	Why are you interested in going into personnel work?
Joseph:	I'm driving a taxi now, but it's only temporary until I can find a more interesting and <u>fulfilling</u> position.
Mrs. Mitchell:	What makes you think you would be good at this job?
Joseph:	Well, the ad said "formal training offered," and I know I could learn how to do the work. I'm a very good worker.
Mrs. Mitchell:	Tell me, have you had any sales experience?
Joseph:	No, I haven't.
Mrs. Mitchell:	Well, we're looking for people who have a certain kind of personality, who are <u>outgoing</u>. We don't exactly sell a <u>product</u>, but we sell a <u>service</u>.
Joseph:	Oh, I see.
Mrs. Mitchell:	That is why we feel a <u>sales</u> personality is very important.
Joseph:	Well, don't you teach that in your training?
Mrs. Mitchell:	In a way we do, but you have to have a certain natural ability to talk to people. Look, Mr. Szeleskiewicz, why don't you give me a number where you can be reached during the day? We will be <u>screening</u> people on the phone all week, and we will call certain applicants back for interviews.
Joseph:	O.K. This is my sister's number, and she's always at home, so you can leave a message for me. 638-4902.

Mrs. Mitchell: That's 638-4902. Fine, and thank you very much for calling.

Joseph: Thank you. Goodbye.

What Happened?

Write T *if the sentence is true,* F *if it is false.*

_____ 1. Joseph is calling about a job as personnel manager.

_____ 2. In his country he received a teaching degree.

_____ 3. Mrs. Mitchell feels that a sales personality is important for everyone in the training program.

_____ 4. Joseph has been in the United States for eight months.

_____ 5. A person with a sales personality is outgoing.

_____ 6. Joseph is happy with his present position.

Hidden Meanings

Think about the following questions carefully before discussing in class. If necessary, refer to the story.

1. Why does the receptionist ask, "Which job are you inquiring about and in which paper did you see it?"

2. Why does Joseph feel that his present job is temporary?

3. Do you think Mrs. Mitchell will call Joseph again? Why or why not?

4. Why did Mrs. Mitchell think it was important to mention that they didn't sell a product, but a service?

Finding the Definition

Circle the letter of the expression that has the same meaning as the underlined word or words.

1. "I would like to arrange for an interview."
   a. have

b. ask for

c. make an appointment for

2. "Which job are you <u>inquiring</u> about?"
   a. talking
   b. asking
   c. giving information

3. His taxi-driving job was not <u>fulfilling</u> to a person with his background.
   a. helpful
   b. satisfying
   c. necessary

4. She has a lot of experience in <u>sales</u>.
   a. selling
   b. shipping
   c. statistics

5. With his <u>outgoing</u> personality, he made friends easily.
   a. sociable
   b. shy
   c. controlled

6. "Please leave a number where you can be <u>reached</u> during the day."
   a. touched
   b. contacted
   c. seen

Finding the Word

Complete each statement using one of the vocabulary words underlined in the text.

1. A person who is being trained for a job is a _____

   _____ .

2. Interviewing many applicants to choose one or a few is called

   _____ .

3. Your education and experience is your _____

   _____ .

4. The field of working with employees or of obtaining jobs for applicants is called _____.

Understanding Words

Which statement is a good example of the meaning of the vocabulary word? Circle A or B.

1. background
   A. "I grew up in Colombia, attended the University of Bogota, and I taught primary school for three years."
   B. "I came to the United States a year ago, and I have been living in New Jersey since I arrived."

2. fulfilling
   A. "I cannot keep my mind on my work; it gives me nothing with which to satisfy my soul."
   B. "I enjoy this job; there is always something new to think about, and I can use all my abilities."

3. screening
   A. "Miss Brown, tell every applicant who calls that there will be a general interview on Tuesday at 10:00 A.M."
   B. "I have interviewed twenty applicants and I will call six of them back for a second interview."

4. outgoing
   A. "I love parties, and I enjoy talking to people."
   B. "I like to go out walking by myself in order to think."

5. switch
   A. "The line is busy. Can you call back later?"
   B. "Hold on, please. I'll transfer your call."

Look at these question forms.

		John	studies	in the library	every evening.
	Does	John	study	in the library	every evening?
Where	does	John	study		every evening?
When	does	John	study	in the library?	
Why	does	John	study	in the library	every evening?
		She	came	to the U.S.	by plane.
	Did	she	come	to the U.S.	by plane?
How	did	she	come	to the U.S.?	

A. *Change the following statements to yes/no questions.*

B. *Ask a question with* What, When, Where, Why *or* How *about the underlined words.*

    Example: Rick saw the ad in the *Evening Star*.

                A. Did Rick see the ad in the *Evening Star*?

                B. Where did Rick see the ad?

1. Howard attended the university from 1960 to 1964.

    A. _____

    B. _____

2. Rosa called about the ad in the News.

    A. _____

    B. _____

3. He had sales experience in Chile.

    A. _____

    B. _____

4. Myron's office is located <u>in the midtown area</u>.

   A. _____

   B. _____

5. The company makes <u>electronic equipment</u>.

   A. _____

   B. _____

6. She wants you to start <u>immediately</u>.

   A. _____

   B. _____

Say It This Way

I am interested in (books).
I am interested in (reading).

I am good at (soccer).
I am good at (organizing).

Answer these questions.

1. What are you interested in?

   _____

2. What are you good at?

   _____

3. What do you enjoy?

   _____

   Ask another student the same questions; then tell the class about your partner.

Communicating by telephone is more difficult than speaking face to face. We do not have the advantages of the nonverbal aspects of communication; we cannot see the movement of the lips. For a non-native person, this makes understanding more difficult.

This problem caused Benjamin Franklin to invent **bifocals** in the year 1784, when he was the American ambassador to France. He found that he could not understand the sounds of French if he could not see the lips of the speakers. When eating in restaurants, he had to keep changing his glasses in order to see his food in front of him and also **converse** with the person across from him. For **convenience**, he invented bifocals.

Unfortunately, no one has yet invented glasses to help the average person see through the telephone receiver. Many of us **suffer** from "telephone fear" when we have to make a job-related call. And, especially, if English is not our native language, we find reasons to **avoid** it. Nevertheless, the telephone is the most powerful job-finding **tool** that we have, and we must learn to use it.

The most important aid in making job-related telephone calls is to be prepared **beforehand**. Before answering an ad, ask yourself:

1. Is the ad from an employment agency or directly from the employer?
2. Does the ad give the name of a contact person?
3. What key words used in describing the job are words that I can use during my telephone conversation?
4. What experience do I have that fits the description in the ad?
5. What information about the company would be helpful to know before I call?
6. What other information do I need to know about the job so I can be prepared to speak?

When making the call, you must be ready to **prove** that you are a person the agency or company should interview. Here are some tips that will help you make a good impression on the telephone.

1. Always have the ad in front of you. Be ready to give the job title and the name and date of the paper in which the ad appeared.

2. Ask the receptionist for the correct pronunciation of the contact's name and his or her job title.
3. Be ready to answer why the job interests you.
4. Mention your relevant experience, education, and personal strengths.
5. Be ready to state when you are available for interviews.
6. Write down the name and address of the company, and the name and phone number of the person you are speaking with.

Glossed Words

bifocals	type of eyeglasses used for both near and distant vision
(to) **converse**	(to) talk
convenience	personal comfort
(to) **suffer**	(to) feel pain or discomfort
(to) **avoid**	(to) stay away from
tool	instrument to help in performing a job
beforehand	in advance
(to) **prove**	(to) confirm

What's It All About?

Answer the following questions with your teacher or in writing on a separate sheet of paper.

1. Why is telephone communication more difficult than speaking face to face?

2. What are bifocals? Who invented them? When?

3. Why are bifocals convenient?

4. What helps a person the most in making job-related phone calls?

5. What are four questions you should be prepared to answer when you make a job-related phone call?

Discuss the following questions with a partner, in a small group, or in a large group with your teacher.

1. What do you find most difficult when talking on the telephone?

2. Have you ever made a telephone call in answer to an ad from the newspaper? What was the result of the call?

Answer the following questions about each ad by writing out the abbreviated word.

FASHION $17,000 Secy
Prof'l assistant needed by Vice
Pres of classic retail operation.
Asst in New Product Division.
Exposure to all areas of mer-
chandising, deal with buyers,
vendors, etc. TYPE 60.

1. What is the actual title of the position?

2. What kind of assistant is needed?

BANKING COLLEGE $20,000
V.P. of int'l bank seeks admin
asst with flexibility to handle
numerous projects. 3+ yrs exp
in a corporate environment
req'd. Oppty to learn word
processing. TYPE 70 + STEN.

1. What is the actual title of the position?

2. What kind of bank is it?

3. What is "3+ yrs exp."?

WORD PROC $16,300
Use your knowl of IBM Text
Pak equipment to get involved
at company that deals with
the medical profession. Dicta
equip a +. Great benefits!

1. What is "WORD PROC"?

2. What is "equip"?

Coll Grad   never a fee $13K
MATH MAJOR
Work as stat asst at mdtn mktg firm. No typg. Excel bnfts. Career oppty.
Carter Agency, 976-8012

1. What is a "stat asst"?

2. Where is it located?

3. What kind of firm is it?

4. What is not required?

PART TIME BOOKKEEPER
Approx 8 hr/wk. Liberal pay.
Reply F5489
Retail co. TIMES 25903

1. How much time is involved on this job?

P/T GAL/G FRI 10-3, 5 days a week.
$6Hr. Resume to Mitchell-Avon Co.
2105 New Country Road, Rm. 2020

1. What is "P/T"?

2. What is "GAL/G FRI"?

Think of a job that you would like to have and in the space below write a classified ad using the list of abbreviations that follows.

Job Title: _____

Help Wanted

Want ads sometimes contain confusing abbreviations. Here are many abbreviations, spelled out. Notice how the abbreviations are made by changing the original word: removing vowels, dropping syllables, using the first letter only, etc.

A-1: the best, good experience
AAS: Associate in Applied Arts or Sciences
Acct: Accountant
admin: administrative
Agt: Agent
Ag, Agcy: Agency
an: analog
approx: approximately
AS: Associate degree
Asmblr, Ass: Assembler
Asmbly, Ass: Assembly
Asst: assistant
att: attendant
avail, avbl: available
Avg: average
BA: Bachelor of Arts
BA: Business Administration
bd: board
bens: benefits
bet: between
bkgrnd, bkrnd: background
bkpr: bookkeeper
blprts: blueprints
Box . . . this newspaper: send to address of newspaper listed at beginning of Help Wanted—Blind Box Notice
BS: Bachelor of Science
CAM: Computer Aided Manufacturing
CAD: Computer Aided Design
cert: certified, certificate
ChE: Chemical Engineer
Civ: Civil
Civ/Serv: Civil Service
clk: clerk

CNC: Computerized Numerical Control
coll: college
coll/grad: college graduate
comm: commission
comp: components
comp: computers
comp/op: computer operator
con, const: construction
debugging: find and correct problem
deg: degree
dept.: department
dig: digital
dir: director
DOE: depends on experience
dwtn: downtown
Ed: education
EE: electrical engineer
elec: electrical
Engr: Engineer
E O E: equal opportunity employer
equip: equipment
equiv: equivalent
est: estimator, estimating
excel: excellent
Exec: executive
exp, exper: experience
ext: extension (telephone)
f/c: file clerk
fin: financial
flex: flexible
FLH: fast long hand
f/p, f/pd: fee paid
f/t: fulltime
gd: good

gen, gen'l: general
G/F: gal friday
hr, hrs: hours
hs, hsg: high school graduate
hskpr: housekeeper
HVAC: heating, ventilation, air
    conditioning
ID: identification
I E: industrial engineer
imm: immediately
ind: industrial
indiv: individual
insp: inspector/inspection
interface: meet with, inter-
    mediary, liason
int'l: international
Jr.: junior
K: thousand (9K means
    salary will be $9,000)
knowl: knowledge
Lab: laboratory
lrn: learn
lic: license, licensed
loc: location
L P N: Licensed Practical Nurse
MA: Master of Arts
mach: machine
maint: maintenance
mdtn: midtown
ME: mechanical or manu-
    facturing engineer
mech: mechanic
metro area: metropolitan area
M/F: male/female
mfg: manufacturing
mgmt, mgt: management
mgr: manager
min: minimum
mktg: marketing
MRP: material requirement
    planning or manufacturing
    resource planning
MS: Master of Science
MSW: Master of Social Work
MT: medical technologist
mtg, mtgs: meeting, meetings
MTM: method, time, and motion

mo: month
nat, natl: national
NC: numerical control
nec: necessary
ofc: office
op: operator
opp, oppty: opportunity
o.t.: overtime
PCB: printed circuit board
per, prsn: person
PERT: program evaluation
    and review techniques
Ph.D.: Doctor of Philosophy
pos: position
pref: prefer
pres: president
pro: professional
p/t: parttime
Q A: Quality Assurance
Q C: Quality Control
R & D: research and devel-
    opment
rep: represent, representative
req, reqs: requires
resp: responsible
rf: radio frequency
rm: room
R N: Registered Nurse
sal: salary
sec: secretary
sect'l: secretarial
serv: service
set-up: prepare machines
s/h, shthd: shorthand
sit: situation
spec: specialist
specs: specifications
Sr: senior
SRF: send resume first
SS: social security
state of the art: knowledge
    of up-to-date, newest spe-
    cialized information for
    particular field
sten: stenography
sup, supvsry: supervisory
sub: substitute

subr, subn: suburbs, suburban
swbd: switchboard
tech: technician
temp: temporary
transp: transportation
trouble shoot: track down,
   locate problem
typ, tpng: typing
UHF: ultra high frequency

uptn: uptown
VHF: very high frequency
VP: vice president
with drive: ambitious
wk: week
word proc: word processing
wpm: words per minute
w/wo: with/without
yr: year

Talking about Yourself

One of the most difficult but most important things to be able to do on any interview is to speak positively about your skills and personal traits without sounding egotistic or artificial. Read the following statements.

Elena: I'm a responsible person. I take my work very seriously. I'm in excellent health and rarely miss a day of work. My child is well taken care of; she's in nursery school, and I have a mature woman who picks her up and takes care of her in the afternoon.

Mark: Experience? Let me think a minute. . . . Well, there was a job with the import company. That was just a trainee position, but I did do sort of the same thing as this job requires . . . that was last October . . . or was it November. . . ?

Pat: I have never done this type of work before, but I have worked with similar equipment, and I learn very quickly. I'm a hard worker, and I know that I can do this job.

Ronnie: I'm interested in a position where I can use all of my skills. I'm determined not to take just any job. I want to be a manager within two years, if not here, then in some other company.

How would you react to these statements? Who would you want to have as an employee?

Choose a partner in the classroom—someone you feel comfortable with. Practice talking about yourself in a positive way.

Person A: Tell me about yourself.

Person B: I can . . .
           In the past I have . . .
           I am the type of person who . . .
               because . . .

Discussion

Did you feel comfortable or uncomfortable talking about yourself? What difficulties did you have, if any?

Telephoning in Response to a Want Ad

Look through the want ads section of a newspaper and find a job that interests you and that you think you are qualified for.

1. Prepare yourself by answering questions 1, 3, 4, 5, and 6 on page 69. Then bring the ad to class.
2. Work in groups of three. Each person will take turns playing the role of the applicant, the employer, and the observer. The employer will look at the applicant's newspaper ad and take a few minutes to decide what the job is and what kind of person is needed. The employer should consider: (a) salary, (b) hours, (c) responsibilities of the job, (d) the applicant's skills, educational background, and personal strengths, and (e) starting date.

When the employer is ready, the applicant and the employer will act out the telephone conversation. While they are acting, the observer will listen and evaluate the interview. The observer should answer these questions.

1. Did they greet each other properly?
2. Was the applicant prepared?
3. Was the applicant successful in getting all the information he or she needed?
4. Was the prospective employer clear in giving information? Did he or she indicate what kind of person was needed?

5. Did the applicant answer questions appropriately? Did he or she sound confident? Why or why not?

Read this example of telephoning to set up an interview for information.

Receptionist:	Connors, Snelling, and Mitchell. May I help you?
Caller:	Yes, I would like to speak to Mr. Michaels, please.
Receptionist:	Do you have an extension for him?
Caller:	No, I don't, but I know he is in the accounting department.
Receptionist:	Hold on, please. I'll ring that department.
Caller:	Thank you.
Secretary:	Accounting, Miss Rogers.
Caller:	Mr. Michaels, please.
Secretary:	Mr. Michaels is on the other line at the moment. May I tell him who's calling?
Caller:	This is _____. Mrs. Radcliff suggested that I call him.
Secretary:	Will you hold on or would you like to leave a message?
Caller:	I'll hold on, thank you. (*after a pause*)
Mr. Michaels:	Tom Michaels speaking; can I help you?
Caller:	Yes, my name is _____. A mutual friend of ours, Jean Radcliff, referred me to you. I am interested in changing careers, and she thought you would be a valuable source of information for me.
Mr. Michaels:	Mrs. Radcliff, of course. How can I help you?
Caller:	I would like very much to come up and speak with you. Would you be willing to give me a few minutes of your time?
Mr. Michaels:	Well, my schedule is a little tight. When were you thinking of meeting?
Caller:	Whenever it is convenient for you.
Mr. Michaels:	Well, can you make it after five o'clock some day next week?
Caller:	Yes, I can.

Mr. Michaels:	Fine, then, how is 5:15, Wednesday, at my office?
Caller:	Next Wednesday at 5:15 is fine. Thank you very much, Mr. Michaels.
Mr. Michaels:	You're welcome. Hold on—my secretary will give you directions.
Caller:	Thank you. See you Wednesday.

6

RÉSUMÉS: SIMON'S STORY

Another day of no responses. Simon found nothing in his mailbox but the usual junk mail and bills. So much unwanted mail and not one of the letters he was hoping to receive! Two weeks ago, Simon had optimistically sent out twenty résumés to various engineering companies. These were companies that he knew worked in his field. He had checked them in the *Thomas Register* and in the *New York State Industrial Directory*. He had even looked up the companies in the *Million Dollar Directory*, which he had consulted at the public library. But still he had received no responses. What was wrong with him?

Simon was feeling very discouraged. Maybe his friend Michael was on the right track. Michael was always telling him, "It's all in how you package your skills and experience. It's all in how you sell yourself." Michael had attended an evening course at the university called "How to Package Your Skills in Today's Market," and since then he had been speaking a language Simon couldn't understand. Simon felt confused and frustrated. He went for a long walk to think about his problems.

"How many ways can there be," he thought, "of talking about my skills and experience? What is all this nonsense about packaging and selling yourself? Am I a box of cornflakes for someone to buy off the shelf? Or am I an experienced, skilled engineer?" He had difficulty understanding this. Where he came from, the person with the right qualifications was matched with the right job. In America, everything seemed to be a contest.

That same afternoon, while glancing through the newspaper, Simon saw an ad for a one-day seminar offered by a career counseling organization. The course was called "How to Package Your-self in Today's Job Market." The seminar would explain how to organize a résumé in the best possible way, as well as how to compose a good cover letter to send with the résumé. Simon was interested and curious, in spite of himself. He decided to look into it. Could they possibly tell him something about himself that he didn't already know?

Answer the following questions.

1. What kind of letter was Simon waiting for?

   _____

2. What did he find in his mailbox?

   _____

3. Where did Simon check for the names of companies in his field?

   _____

4. What did Simon think about his friend Michael?

   _____

5. What was the name of the seminar that Simon decided to take?

   _____

Think about the following questions carefully before discussing in class. If necessary, refer to the story.

1. Why do you think Simon had not received any responses from the companies he wrote to?

2. What did his friend Michael mean when he said, "It's all in how you package your skills and experience"?

3. Why did Simon feel like a "package of cornflakes"?

4. What do you think the career counseling organization meant by "How to Sell Yourself in Today's Job Market"?

Finding
the Definition

Circle the letter of the expression that has the same meaning as the underlined word or words.

1. Simon found the usual junk mail in his mail box.
   a. useful mail
   b. useless mail
   c. used mail

2. He consulted the *Million Dollar Directory* in the library.
   a. took out
   b. looked for information in
   c. compared

3. Simon mailed his résumé with a cover letter attached.
   a. a letter accompanying a résumé
   b. a thank-you letter
   c. an invitation

4. He thought this talk about "selling yourself" was a lot of nonsense.
   a. words without meaning
   b. sensible advice
   c. wasted time

5. They told him how to compose a cover letter.
   a. type
   b. make up
   c. mail

Finding
the Word

Complete each statement using one of the vocabulary words underlined in the text.

1. A competition to win a prize or reward is called a _____

   _____ .

2. A class or workshop that provides students the opportunity for

   advanced discussion of a subject is a _____ .

3. Companies that deal with design and production specifications are called _____ companies.

4. An organization that helps people discover the right job is an organization specializing in _____ .

Which statement is a good example of the meaning of the vocabulary word? Circle A or B.

1. <u>optimistic</u>
   A. "Everything's going to be fine; don't worry."
   B. "I'd love to take a walk, but it's raining."

2. <u>nonsense</u>
   A. "When I'm not near the one I love, I love the one I'm near."
   B. "Over the moon, flippety flop, red and green and blue."

3. <u>selling yourself</u>
   A. "I saved my previous employers 20 percent in fuel expenses. I can do the same for you. Let me show you how."
   B. "I think I can learn to do this job, although I haven't worked with this type of equipment specifically."

4. <u>consult</u>
   A. "Can you tell me how to find some information about companies that want electronic engineers?"
   B. "I'd like to tell you something interesting that I heard today."

Learning through Practice: Past Tense Affirmative and Negative Statements

Look at the following sentences.

I		smoked	two cigarettes yesterday.
I	didn't	smoke	a pipe.
I		walked	to work yesterday.
I	didn't	walk	to work this morning.
I		spoke	to the vice president.
I	didn't	speak	to the president.

For the past tense of regular verbs add *-d* or *-ed* to the infinitive form of the verb. See list that follows for common irregular verbs. In the negative, use *didn't* with the infinitive form of the verb.

Past Tense Changes i *to* a
Past Participle Changes i *to* u

begin	began	begun
drink	drank	drunk
ring	rang	rung
sing	sang	sung
swim	swam	swum

Other Irregular Verbs

be	was/were	been
blow	blew	blown
break	broke	broken
choose	chose	chosen
do	did	done
drive	drove	driven
eat	ate	eaten
fly	flew	flown
fall	fell	fallen
forget	forgot	forgotten
get	got	gotten/got
give	gave	given
go	went	gone

grow	grew	grown
know	knew	known
lie	lay	lain
ride	rode	ridden
rise	rose	risen
see	saw	seen
speak	spoke	spoken
take	took	taken
throw	threw	thrown
wear	wore	worn
write	wrote	written

Verbs Whose Three Forms Are Alike in Spelling

cost	cost	cost
cut	cut	cut
hurt	hurt	hurt
put	put	put
read	read	read

Past Tense and Past Participle ending in d

have	had	had
hear	heard	heard
lay	laid	laid
make	made	made
pay	paid	paid
say	said	said
sell	sold	sold
tell	told	told

Past Tense and Past Participle ending in t

bring	brought	brought
build	built	built
buy	bought	bought
catch	caught	caught
feel	felt	felt
keep	kept	kept
leave	left	left
lend	lent	lent

lose	lost	lost
send	sent	sent
sleep	slept	slept
spend	spent	spent
teach	taught	taught
think	thought	thought

Past Tense and Past Participle with Internal Vowel Change

come	came	come
find	found	found
hold	held	held
meet	met	met
run	ran	run
sit	sat	sat
stand	stood	stood
win	won	won

Read the following paragraph and change all the verbs in parentheses to the past tense.

Konstantin's Story

When I (come)_____ here eleven years ago, I (know)_____ only three words: "No speak English." So I (start)_____ washing dishes. I (take)_____ any job to survive, and everybody (say)_____ to me, "You were an engineer? Forget about it. You'll never get a job as an engineer." Well, you have to know one thing. If you (are)_____ a good engineer where you came from, you'll be a good engineer here, if you know what you want, and if you know the right way to get to your position. Unfortunately, I (suffer)_____ terribly, because I (not, have)_____ anyone to show me how. I (work)_____ very hard on my

English, and finally I (get)_____ a job as an assistant engineer in Connecticut. Can you imagine, a field engineer who (can't)_____ speak English? I (am) _____ the first one in the United States.

At the beginning I (send)_____ out thousands of résumés, and I (not, get)_____ an answer. You know why? Because I (not, know)_____ how to write a résumé. You know, in America there is a "marketplace." If you don't fit into what they need, they don't take you. In Rumania we (have)_____ to do everything—low-voltage, high voltage, electric, mechanical. So I (put) _____ in my résumé everything that I really did. But in America if they see everything in the résumé, they throw it in the garbage because they want you to specialize in one thing. Then I (get)_____ smart. I started to write *three* résumés. I (write)_____ résumé number one, in which I (swear)_____ that all my life I did electrical engineering, résumé number two, in which I (swear)_____ that all my life I did electronic engineering, and résumé number three, in which I (swear)_____ that all my life I did drilling engineering. And each one (is)_____ true! I (keep)_____ a list, because I (not, want)_____ to send two different résumés to the same company. Résumés are a catastrophe.

Say It This Way

From the list below, choose an idiom that has the same meaning as the underlined phrase, and rewrite the complete sentence.

to look up
to look into
to sell yourself
on the right track
to package your skills
in spite of myself

1. It's necessary <u>to convince the employer that you would be a valuable employee</u>.

   _____

   _____

2. Did you <u>find the meaning of</u> the word in the dictionary?

   _____

   _____

3. You don't have the right answer yet, but you're <u>thinking in the right direction</u>.

   _____

   _____

4. She really has learned how to <u>present her qualifications in an attractive way</u>.

   _____

   _____

5. I have to <u>investigate</u> this matter.

   _____

   _____

6. <u>Against my will</u>, I was curious about the strange advertisement in the newspaper.

   _____

   _____

The word *résumé* is a French word, now used in English, that means **summary**. In the American job market, you must **represent** yourself on paper. The résumé is your **calling card**. Its purpose is to attract the interest of the prospective employer. It can be your ticket into the interview. That is why people often have more than one résumé. They choose the most **appropriate** one for each job that they apply for.

Your résumé should show the employer how your skills match the job you are applying for. It should give the employer a sense that you would be a good **investment** for the company. To be effective, your résumé should:

1. emphasize your accomplishments—not just your job titles and responsibilities, but also the results you obtained;
2. include only the work experience that is **relevant** to the job you are applying for;
3. be easy to read and not too **wordy**; and
4. have no spelling, grammatical, or typing errors.

There are two basic **formats** for organizing the information about your work experience. The first is ***chronological***. In a chronological résumé, jobs are listed with the most recent first. Your dates of employment, name of employer, and job title are listed in order. This is followed by a statement explaining your accomplishments on the job. The sample on page 92 is a chronological résumé.

The second format is called ***functional***. In a functional résumé, experience and skills are given by job title, without dates or places of employment. This method is useful where the job-seeker has made many changes, is in **transition** from one field to another, or has never worked before. The résumé on page 93 is a functional résumé.

The following is an outline for an effective résumé:

1. *Heading*
   Name, address, and telephone number in the upper left/right hand corner or upper middle of the page. Include zip code and telephone area code.

2. *Professional Objective and Summary*

This can be very important. This is your **goal** around which all other items in the résumé revolve. Include only your immediate goal. Be specific with a job title or a clear description of your area of interest. Sometimes a brief summary of your qualifications is helpful.

3. *Professional Experience*

List by chronology or function, according to what is most appropriate for your background. Give a description of what you did, materials or products used or worked on, your accomplishments, a sample of something **significant** that you did. Use action verbs like *planned, organized, developed,* and *managed.*

4. *Education*

Use the comparable American degrees wherever possible.

5. *Personal Data*

Give your immigration and residence status and state that your employment is authorized. List the languages you are fluent in, making sure to indicate your native language and English!

Be prepared to rewrite your résumé on the basis of information you gain from your first few interviews or contacts. Pay attention to the questions you are asked and any comments about your experience. Use this information to improve your résumé. Remember, your résumé is *you*.

Glossed Words

summary	total or sum in brief form
(to) **represent**	(to) set forth a likeness or image; set forth in words
calling card	small card printed with one's name
appropriate	proper; suitable
investment	commitment of money and other resources (time, training) for a profit

relevant	applicable
wordy	too many words
format	style of printed materials—books, magazines
chronological	listing in order of time (dates)
functional	connected to specific area of work, e.g., sales, finance
transition	movement from one condition, place, or action to another
elements	parts of a whole
goal	objective; an end
significant	important

Chronological Résumé

Kuo Ye Kwon
8265 Sedgwick Avenue, Apt. 6B
Bronx, N.Y. 10463
212-884-4159

OBJECTIVE: To work in a data processing department of a large com-
                  pany as a computer programmer

HARDWARE: Honeywell 62-100, CRT DISCS
                  DISKETTE READER, IBM-S 34

SOFTWARE: COBOL, BASIC, OS JCL

EMPLOYMENT
EXPERIENCE:
10/81-Present   Adelphia University Urban Center
N.Y.C., U.S.A.   Laboratory Assistant
                  ● Helped students in laboratory with problem solving
                    and program writing.

4/80-4/81   E & B Supermarkets, Inc.
Bronx, N.Y.   Assistant Manager
U.S.A.   ● Programmed payroll and sales analysis series.
                  ● Wrote, tested and debugged individual parts of pro-
                    grams.
                  ● Wrote programs for general ledger, payroll, ac-
                    counts payable, and inventory application. These
                    applications involved writing sophisticated rou-
                    tines, data communications, screen layouts, and
                    internal sorting techniques. All programs were
                    written in COBOL.

1975-79   Optical-Mechanical Plant
1966-72   Junior Programmer
Seoul, Korea   Promoted to Programmer
                  ● Programmed series of payroll and statistical analy-
                    ses models for Data Processing Department.
                  ● Responsible for design output, report layout, writ-
                    ing tests, and debugging. All programs as well as
                    sample program documentation were written in COBOL.

EDUCATION: Optical-Mechanical Institute
1960-66   Data Processing department
Seoul, Korea

REFERENCES: Available upon request.

Functional Résumé

(Mr. Mortonki has worked as a tour leader only as a supplement to his full-time job. Now he is interested in changing fields, so it is advantageous to present his experience in a functional format, without showing names and dates of employers.)

Henry Mortonki
13 Francis Terringfield
Glen, Vermont 12345
802-391-6674

Job Objective: Tour Leader and/or Planner

Languages: German, French

Experience:

TOUR   Oriented tour groups to countries and places to be
LEADER: visited; checked passports and visas of partici-
              pants; checked groups into hotels, assigned rooms
and supervised delivery of baggage; organized check-out baggage
counts; provided leadership for unforseen problems; resolved conflicts relating to group interaction and local travel schedules.

TOUR   Determined countries and cities to be visited; se-
PLANNER: cured visa applications where necessary; estab-
              lished deadline for deposit and final payment for
tour; advised participants on passport and visa regulations and necessary health measures; made air and ground travel arrangements and
hotel and restaurant reservations; arranged with local touring organizations for local sightseeing, cultural attractions, and shopping.

RECRUITER: Made film or slide presentations to interested poten-
              tial clients.

Education: PhD Columbia University, 1960 Political Science
              MA Columbia University, 1952
              BA City College NYC   1950 History

Memberships: American Association for the Advancement of Germanic
                 Studies
              Citizen's Exchange Corps
              International Exchange Union

What's It All About?

Answer the following questions with your teacher or in writing on a separate sheet of paper.

1. Why do people often write more than one résumé?

2. What type of résumé format lists jobs with dates starting from the most recent?

3. What type of résumé format does not include dates?

4. What is meant by *professional objective* or *job objective*?

5. When should you be prepared to rewrite your résumé?

Can We Talk?

Discuss the following questions with a partner, in small groups, or in a large group with your teacher.

1. Here are three cereals on a shelf in the supermarket. You can only buy one, so you can't afford to make the wrong choice. What will you think about when deciding which cereal to buy? Consider: brand name, price, ingredients, nutritional value, advertising, packaging, display, etc.

$1.85   95¢   69¢

2. How can you compare examining a product that you are going to buy, to examining the résumé of someone you might hire? Consider the following:

> attractiveness to buyer/employer
> ingredients/qualifications
> value to buyer/employer

3. You are the manager of a department. There is a job opening for an accounting clerk. You have received many résumés for the position, but you have narrowed it down to the three résumés on the following pages. What will you look for when trying to decide which candidate to interview for the position? Use the résumé evaluation guide that follows.

Résumé Evaluation Guide

Consider the following points when evaluating a résumé:

I. *Form*
   a. Is it attractive to the eye in terms of printing, organization of information, and neatness?
   b. Is it easy to read?
   c. Is it free from errors in spelling, punctuation, grammar, typing, and spacing?

II. *Content*
   a. Is the job objective clear?
   b. Does the experience match the job being requested?
   c. Are there gaps in employment?
   d. Is there any irrelevant information (i.e., information that is not related to the job requested)?
   e. Is all the necessary information about education (dates and degrees), employment history (names, locations, dates), and references presented?

Putting It to Work

a. *Look in the newspaper and select a job that you are qualified for and/or would like to have, and write a résumé for it.*
b. *After you have completed your résumé, choose a partner, and critique the positive and negative aspects of each other's résumé. Use the résumé evaluation guide.*

```
                            Marie Beaumarchais
                            1734 Ocean Parkway
                            Chicago, IL 60691
                            312-687-7110


JOB OBJECTIVE:      Assistant bookkeeper or any challenging position in
                    the bookkeeping area that will give me an opportu-
                    nity to utilize my knowledge of accounts receiv-
                    able, accounts payable, bank reconciliations, and
                    payroll.

WORK EXPERIENCE:
Bank of Haiti
  1980-1982         Supervisor of Accounts Payable Department

  1976-1980         In charge of accounts payable, checked invoices
                    against bills, processed checks, kept records up to
                    date, followed up delinquent invoices.

  1974-1976         Figure Clerk: kept track of bank transactions,
                    checked all withdrawals and deposits from all tell-
                    ers, checked that they coincided with the amount of
                    transactions.

  1972-1974         bank teller

  1971-1972         teller trainee

EDUCATION:          Lycee de Haiti, 1970, High School diploma

LANGUAGES:          French (native), English

STATUS:             Employment authorized, immigrant status, citizen-
                    ship expected in 1987
```

Paul Makarovich
1206 Forest St.
San Diego, CA 11824
(213) 451-3039

JOB OBJECTIVE

GOAL: To obtain a position as an accounting clerk or assist-
              ant bookkeeper.

EDUCATION: Brookings University
1979   Certificate in Junior Accounting Training Program.
              Included bookkeeping and accounting procedures:
              Journalizing practical and posting Transactions
              (such transactions as accounts payable, accounts re-
              ceivable, cash receipts, sales, cash payments and
              purchases): bank reconciliations; calculation of
              payroll and payroll taxes, sales tax and rent and oc-
              cupancy tax. The course also included oral and writ-
              ten English, Business English and office practice
              procedures, including typing and use of the adding
              machine.

Special Skills Light typing, adding machine.
1971

Degree   Leningrad University Degree: Slavic Languages.

EMPLOYMENT

1975–1978   Supervisor of Payroll of a technical department.

1973–1975   Executive secretary of the Personnel Department of
              Geology Company.

1971–1973   Scientific assistant of the *Pushkin's House*.

              Employment authorized by the U.S. Immigration Ser-
              vice.

LANGUAGES: Russian (native), English

REFERENCES: Available upon request.

ANTHONY J. MAJORS

12 Oak Drive   Date of Birth: September 21, 1958
New Hyde Park, New York 11040   Marital Status: Single
(516) 352-8350

EXPERIENCE

AUDITING: Concerns having up to sixty million dollars gross sales.
                   Experience with certified audits, SEC clients, EDP sys-
                   tems and statistical analysis.

YEAR END   Including preparation of workpapers, worksheets, and
CLOSINGS: adjusting entries.

FINANCIAL   Preparation of monthly, quarterly, and annual compara-
STATEMENTS: tive balance sheets, income statements, and statements
                   of changes in financial position.

TAXES: Preparation and planning of corporation, partnership,
                   estate, trust, and individual taxes, on the federal,
                   state, and local level. Preparation of payroll taxes,
                   sales taxes, commercial rent, and occupancy taxes.

EMPLOYMENT

1979–
present   Sommer, Abraham and Green, CPA's, New York, NY

1978–1979   Restaino and Cohen, CPA's, Oakland, CA

EDUCATION

1976–1979   University of California at Berkely—B.B.A.—Accounting

                   Pace University—M.B.A.—Taxation
                   Night classes begin in the Fall semester, 1980.

REFERENCES

                   Suitable professional and personal references will be
                   furnished upon request.

7

BUSINESS LETTERS: PETER'S STORY

Asking
for Advice

Gabriela Corelli is a placement counselor in an organization that helps non-native speakers of English find jobs. Peter has been Gabriela's client for a year.

Gabriela: Hello, Peter, I haven't seen you for a while. <u>How are things</u>?

Peter: Well, about the same.

Gabriela: Last semester you told me you were sending out a new letter. Did you have any success with it?

Peter: Not really. I only received some form letters thanking me for applying for the position and telling me that they will keep my résumé on file.

Gabriela: You seem very <u>down</u> today.

Peter: Yes, because I feel I'm really <u>stuck</u> in this low-paying job.

Gabriela: Why do you think you aren't getting any responses?

Peter: I don't know. I've changed my résumé three times and my cover letter twice. I even had my letters especially printed, and I sent out fifty of them.

Gabriela: Why don't you sit down for a moment, and let's take a look at your cover letter.

Gentlemen:

I am interested in an engineering position with your firm in the general area of <u>interplant</u> material handling, outside transportation, and industrial <u>site</u> development for machine-construction <u>plants</u>.

One of my major skills is in designing plant projects that are <u>cost efficient</u>. I was responsible for large scale planning that used new techniques which <u>reduced</u> construction costs of buildings, roads, and <u>utilities</u> by 10 to 50 percent.

I have had twenty-five years experience working with a <u>consulting</u> engineering organization in the Soviet Union. I began as an engineer with the equivalent of a <u>master's degree</u> in civil engineering, moving on through the engineering ranks to become the senior consulting engineer for industrial site development and transportation systems being developed in the automotive industries.

During the last twelve years, I took part in developing some of the most important automotive plants built in the USSR. This involved a significant cooperation with Western firms, including Fiat (for the Togliatti Car Complex), Renault (for the Moscow Car Plant), and with Swindell-Dressler (for the Kamaz Truck Complex).

Thank you for your consideration.

                                        Sincerely yours,

                                        Peter _____

Gabriela:	This is much better than the last letter you showed me.
Peter:	Thank you. Do you think it's too long or too wordy?
Gabriela:	Well, maybe, but your grammar has really improved and the letter is more focused and to the point.
Peter:	Do you have any other suggestions?
Gabriela:	Yes. It also needs a closing sentence because it ends too abruptly. And one other question . . . is this for a specific job?
Peter:	Yes.
Gabriela:	Then using a form letter can be a disadvantage. It's better to send it to a specific person in that company. I have an appointment in a few moments, but why don't you come back after lunch and we'll talk more about it.

What Happened?

Write T *if the sentence is true,* F *if it is false.*

_____ 1. Peter is discontented with his present job.

_____ 2. He sent out fifty form letters with his résumé.

_____ 3. He received some responses from employers who were interested.

_____ 4. He changed his résumé twice.

_____ 5. Ms. Corelli is a potential employer for Peter.

_____ 6. Some companies are keeping Peter's résumé on file.

_____ 7. A cover letter is the same as a letter of application.

_____ 8. Peter feels he will never get a better job.

Hidden Meanings

Think about the following questions carefully before discussing in class. If necessary, refer to the story.

1. Why would a company keep your résumé on file?

2. Why did Gabriela suggest that Peter send the letter to a specific person rather than send a form letter?

3. Why did Peter feel he could drop in without an appointment?

1. Why do you think Peter wasn't getting any responses?

2. Did you find the letter too long?

3. Is all the information necessary?

4. Is there anything you think that should be in the letter that isn't there?

Circle the letter of the expression that has the same meaning as the underlined word or words.

1. He did not receive any <u>responses</u> to his letter.
   a. answers
   b. stamps
   c. information

2. Form letters are convenient; however, they have some <u>disadvantages</u>.
   a. mistakes
   b. positive aspects
   c. negative aspects

3. I worked with a <u>consulting</u> engineering organization.
   a. providing information
   b. construction
   c. government

4. We never know what they are doing at the other factories. We need better <u>interplant</u> communication.
   a. between plants
   b. inside of one factory
   c. outer space

5. Last year we <u>reduced</u> costs from $2 million to $1.75 million.
   a. raised
   b. lowered
   c. reorganized

Finding
the Word

Complete each statement using one of the vocabulary words underlined in the text.

1. In America, the next educational degree after a bachelor's degree is a _____.

2. A specific piece of land is called a _____.

3. Another term for factory is _____.

4. Electricity, water supply, and telephone service are

    _____.

5. Something that gives good results for money spent is

    _____.

Understanding
Words

Which statement is a good example of the meaning of the vocabulary word? Circle A or B.

1. down
   A. "Let's not go to the movies today. Let's just stay home and relax."
   B. "What a miserable interview I just had! I'm sick and tired of looking for a job."

2. wordy
   A. "I look forward to hearing from you in regard to possible employment."
   B. "I hope that at your convenience you will respond to my letter and that we can set up an appointment in the near future, since I am extremely interested in working for your company."

3. abrupt
   A. "I greatly appreciate your coming in to see us this morning. It's been a pleasure talking with you. As we discussed, I'll be in touch with you."
   B. "You certainly have a very interesting background. We have to stop now because I have another appointment."

The gerund is the *-ing* form of the verb used as a noun in the subject or object position of a sentence. It is often followed by another noun.

Look at the following sentences.

	Gerund (-ing) as object
I was responsible for One of my major skills is I have had 3 years of experience	*typing* statistical reports.
Gerund (-ing) as subject *Typing* statistical reports	is something I do well. is one of my best skills. is a job I really enjoy.

Rewrite the sentence, which is in the past tense, using the gerund in the object and subject position.

Example: I *typed* legal documents.

> I was responsible for *typing* legal documents.
> One of my major skills is *typing* legal documents.
> I have had 3 years of experience *typing* legal documents.
> *Typing* legal documents is something I do well.
> *Typing* legal documents is one of my best skills.
> *Typing* legal documents is a job I really enjoy.

1. I supervised a large group.

   _____

   _____

   _____

   _____

   _____

   _____

2. I designed software for micro-computers.

   _____

   _____

   _____

   _____

   _____

3. I taught mathematics in primary school.

   _____

   _____

   _____

   _____

   _____

   _____

Say It This Way

Match the idioms in Column A with the definitions in Column B.

Column A	Column B
a. to the point	____ in the records
b. to be stuck (in a job)	____ to glance
c. how are things?	____ direct, clear

d. on file

_____ to be trapped, unable to advance

e. to take a look

_____ how's everything with you?

A letter of application is necessary in the following situations: (a) when answering a specific ad from the newspaper, (b) when writing to a specific person whose name you got from someone else, and (c) when writing to a specific company that you feel is a good place for you to get a job.

The letter has one main objective: to interest the employer in your qualifications so you will get an interview. It should accompany either a résumé or a completed application form.

A letter of application should be prepared very carefully. It can decide whether an employer will pass it on to the personnel department with the note, "This looks **worth** a **follow-up**," or will quietly drop it into the nearest wastebasket. Employers receive many letters and cannot pay attention to all of them; if you want yours to "set you apart," or to attract attention, observe the following rules.

1. Whenever possible, address your letter by name to the appropriate person in the company.
2. Use standard-size (8 1/2" × 11"), good-quality white **bond paper**.
3. Type the letter or have it typed. Make sure there are no errors!
4. Be very careful with spelling and punctuation. If you are not sure of the spelling or precise meaning of a word, consult the dictionary, or a friend, or use a word you feel sure about.
5. Be brief—your letter should take up no more than a page. Businesslike letters will receive more attention. Three paragraphs is an ideal length.
6. In your first paragraph, **mention** the job you are applying for and where you saw it advertised. If you are not applying for a specific job, identify yourself, mention who **referred** you, if anyone, and why you are applying to this company.

7. In the second paragraph, state (a) why you think you are qualified for this job; (b) what **contribution** you can make to this company; and (c) any **related** work experience. If in the past you have worked for a good company, it is important to mention that. Tell how many years of experience you have. Then, write one statement to show that you understand what the company you are writing to does (example: "Fischer-Price is one of the largest manufacturers of quality creative toys in the U.S.") and add that you are enclosing a résumé. Mention your most outstanding qualification as stated on the enclosed résumé.

8. The closing paragraph should ask for an interview and say where and when you can be reached. You may suggest that you will phone for an interview. Make sure you telephone the company **within** a week after mailing the letter.

9. Keep a copy of every letter you send.

Glossed Words

worth	value; merit
follow-up	a second or immediate following action
bond paper	strong paper used for business letters
(to) **mention**	(to) inform; speak of briefly
(to) **refer**	(to) send or direct for information
contribution	something one gives to a situation
related	connected
within	in the limits of a specific time

What's It All About?

Answer the following questions with your teacher or in writing on a separate sheet of paper.

1. Why is it important to prepare a cover letter carefully?

2. What kind of letter will receive the most attention?

3. How many paragraphs should a cover letter contain?

108

4. How soon should you telephone after sending a letter?

5. What should you always keep for your file?

Can We Talk?

Discuss the following questions with a partner, in small groups, or in a large group with your teacher.

1. How does competition in the job market affect the employer's attitude toward your letter?

2. Read the letters below, and discuss the good and bad points of each. Use as a guide the evaluation questions that follow each letter.

Dear Sir;

I am currently unemployed and am looking for a job as manager in a toy manufacturing company.

As you can see from my enclosed résumé, I have exten-sive experience in toy companies, and know all aspects of production. In the past, I have also supervised six-teen people in a hat manufacturing company, as well as being head cashier for a large supermarket.

I have heard many good things about your company, and would like very much to work for you.

I look forward to hearing from you in order to set up an interview.

Very truly yours,

Edward Bright

Edward Bright

---

1. Is the opening sentence appropriate? Why or why not?

2. Is all the information in the second paragraph relevant?

```
To Whom It May Concern:

Several months ago I emigrated from
_____ to the United States. Since my
arrival I have been engaged in a comprehensive English
course to prepare myself for employment in my field.

I would like to work in your organization because your
activities very closely parallel my professional
background and experience. I have designed, drafted,
and tested machinery for the petroleum and chemical
industries. Since I am quite anxious to secure related
work, my salary requirements are open.

I have attached a copy of my résumé for your consider-
ation and would appreciate information regarding
available positions. I would be happy to discuss this
in an interview at your convenience.


                              Sincerely,



                              Michaela Lirtsman
Encl.
```

Evaluation

1. Look at the third sentence in the second paragraph. When might this statement be appropriate? Not appropriate?

2. In general, is this a good or a bad letter?

425 Riverside Drive
Baton Rouge, LA 19235

August 2, 1982

P.O. Box 18353
Baton Rouge, LA 19228

Dear Sir or Madam;

I saw your ad for a hotel clerk in the Louisiana Traveler, and I wish to apply for the position.

I graduated from the Huey Long High School in Baton Rouge and in my senior year I took a number of business and accounting courses. Last year I worked part time as a bellhop and assisted the night manager at the Holiday Inn in Baton Rouge. I am enclosing my résumé, giving details of my responsibilities in that job. I am a serious and reliable worker, and can furnish recommendations upon request.

I look forward to having an interview with you in order to discuss the position and my qualifications. You can reach me any evening between 7 and 10 P.M. at 483-1210.

Thank you for your consideration.

Sincerely yours,

Fred Fanning

Fred Fanning

Encl.

Evaluation
1. What, if anything, would you change in this letter?

Make up cover letters:

a. to someone at a specific company that you would like to work for. You know this company through either their product or their service.
b. to someone to whom you have been recommended.
c. in response to an ad from a newspaper, to a company where you do not know anyone.

Use the format shown on pages 113 and 114 for your letter and envelope.

Sample Openings and Closings to Cover Letters

Openings

Attached you will find my résumé.

I am looking for a position as . . .

I am responding to your ad in the Sunday newspaper for the position of . . .

At the suggestion of Mr. (or Ms.) _____ , I am enclosing my résumé for the position of . . .

Closings

I am looking forward to hearing from you.

I will be in touch in the near future to discuss . . .

I would very much appreciate an interview at your convenience.

I will call next week to set up an appointment.

Letter of Application Format

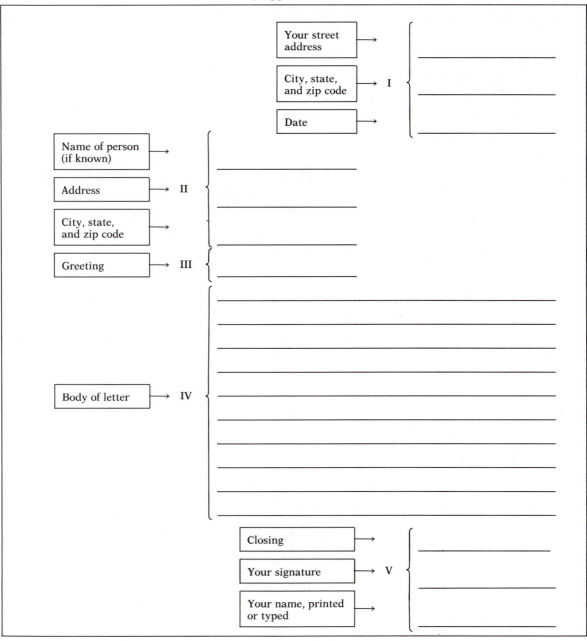

Viola Martino
4732 Flatwoods Avenue
St. Paul, MN 55111

YWCA of the City of Minneapolis
610 Lexington Avenue
Minneapolis, MN 55422

8

APPLICATIONS AND FORMS: ALI'S STORY

"I will never be able to answer all these questions," thought Ali as he stared at the two-page job application form. "I don't even remember some of these dates," he thought, as he looked it over more closely. He looked around the waiting room of the employment agency and realized that everyone had the same troubled expression on his or her face. He laughed to himself, realizing that they were all in the same boat. "Well," he decided, "the only way to get through this application is to go ahead and fill it out the best way I can." He made himself comfortable and began writing in all the details.

Before reading Ali's application, go over the following terms with your teacher and be sure you understand them all:

Personal	Education
ailment	academic
arrested	college (equal to four years university)
chronic	
convicted	commercial
date of birth*	extra-curricular
ethnic group*	high school
illness	major (subject)
marital status*	minor (subject)
physical disability*	post-graduate
recurrent	preparatory school
references	scholastic average
signature	vocational
violation	

* By law, you do not have to answer these questions, but they appear on most applications.

Work History
date available
duties
employer
immediate supervisor

Expressions
in case of emergency
to file a claim

Affidavit
affirm
authorize
disclosed
foregoing
hereby
resignation
unfavorably

Military
branch of service
decorations
discharge
draft status
injuries sustained
rank
reserve

APPLICATION FOR EMPLOYMENT
EQUAL OPPORTUNITY EMPLOYER M/F

PERSONAL INFORMATION   PLEASE PRINT

Date **28/8/85**   Social Security No. **189-64-4231**

Name **RAFAN**   **ALI**

| Last | First | Middle |

Present Address **19 SPRING ST.**   **PHILADELPHIA**   **PA**

| Street | City | State | Zip |

Permanent Address

| Street | City | State | Zip |

Phone No. **215-898-4060** Height **1.7** Weight **75** Sex

Date of Birth **31/7/57**   U.S. Citizen or Alien Resident **ALIEN**   Have You Ever Been Convicted of a Crime? **NO**

If Related to Anyone in Our Employ State Name and Department

Referred by

EMPLOYMENT DESIRED

Position **COMPUTER PROGRAMMER**   Date You Can Start **NOW**   Salary Desired

Are You Employed Now? **No**   If So May We Inquire of Your Present Employer?

Have You Ever Applied to This Company Before? **No**   Where   When

EDUCATION

	School Name and Location	Years Attended	Date Graduated	Subjects Studied
Grammar School				
High School				ACAD. COMM. VOC.
College				MAJOR MINOR
Trade, Business or Correspondence School				

Subjects of Special Study or Research Work

What Foreign Languages Do You Speak Fluently? **TURKISH**

Read   Write

Activities Other Than Religious (Civic, Athletic, Etc.)   **PLAYD FUTBOL**

MILITARY

Years of Active Service _____   Decorations Received _____

List Below Last Four Employers, Starting With Most Recent

Date Month and Year	Full Name and Address of Employer	Salary	Position	Reasons for Leaving
From 79 To 81	TAHSIN MANUFACTURING COMPANY ANKARA, TURKEY	350 MO	JUNIOR PROGRAMMER	PERSONAL REASONS DID NOT AGREE WITH MANAGER
From 81 To 83	SABINCI HOLDING ANKARA, TURKEY	13,500	COMPUTER PROGRAMMER	WENT TO AIR FORCE
From To				
From To				

REFERENCES: Give Below the Names of Three Persons Not Related to You, Whom You Have Known At Least One Year.

Name	Address	Business	Years Acquainted
1. ERIK MUSTAFA	49 ELMER DR.	DOCTOR	10
2. ANA KRISTOFF	525 7TH AVE.	ENGLISH TEACHER	6
3. BRIAN MORGAN	19 SPRING ST.	NEIBOR	2

PHYSICAL RECORD

List Any Physical Defects

Were You Ever Injured? **No**   Give Details

Have You Any Defects in Hearing?   In Vision?   In Speech?

In Case of Emergency Notify **HASIM**   **32 WESTPORT BLVD.**

Name   Address   Phone No.

I authorize investigation of all statements contained in this application. I understand that misrepresentation or omission of facts called for is cause for dismissal. Further, I understand and agree that my employment is for no definite period and may, regardless of the date of payment of my wages and salary, be terminated at any time without any previous notice.

Date **28/8/85**   Signature **ALI RAFAN**

DO NOT WRITE BELOW THIS LINE

Interviewed by   Date

REMARKS:

Discrimination because of age, race, creed, color, or sex is prohibited by law. New York City law prohibits discrimination based on physical handicaps.

What Happened?

Write T *if the sentence is true,* F *if it is false.*

____ 1. Ali lives in Pennsylvania.

____ 2. He played soccer in school.

____ 3. He has never been convicted of a felony.

____ 4. His yearly salary in 1981 was $5,000.

____ 5. The name of Ali's former boss is Hasim.

____ 6. His most recent job was with Tahsin Manufacturing Co.

Convert Ali's height and weight, given on the application, to feet and inches, and pounds. Then answer questions 7 and 8.

____ 7. He is five feet, ten inches tall.

____ 8. He weighs 165 pounds.

Hidden Meanings

Think about the following question carefully before discussing in class. If necessary, refer to the story.

Why did everyone in the agency have a troubled expression?

Analyzing the Application

1. What is the abbreviation for the state you live in?_____

2. Is Ali's education listed correctly?

3. Why is it better to use feet, inches, and pounds on an application, rather than meters, centimeters, and kilos?

4. Why did Ali put a question mark in answer to *decorations received*?

5. What was his most recent job?

6. What did Ali write for *salary desired*? Should he have left it blank or should he have written "open"?

7. In answer to *reasons for leaving* a previous job, how do you think the employer interprets an answer like "personal reasons"? Why isn't this a good thing to put on an application? What is a better answer?

8. Did Ali omit anything? Which of these things should not have been omitted?

9. Are any words misspelled?

10. What do you notice about Ali's date of birth?

Finding the Definition

Circle the letter of the expression that has the same meaning as the underlined word or words.

1. That general received four <u>decorations</u> during the war in Vietman.
   a. ornaments
   b. medals
   c. letters

2. The <u>injuries sustained</u> by the police officer during the robbery were not serious.
   a. wounds received
   b. wounds given
   c. arrests made

3. This employee has <u>chronic</u> heart problems and needs to stop working.
   a. artificial
   b. temporary
   c. recurring

4. He was asked for three <u>references</u> on the job application.
   a. names of persons who know you
   b. books
   c. addresses

5. It is <u>a violation</u> to cross the street when the light is red.
   a. breaking the law
   b. permitted
   c. difficult

Finding
the Word

Complete each statement using one of the vocabulary words underlined in the text.

1. Courses taken after completing an advanced degree are called

   _____ _____ studies.

2. Courses pertaining to specific trades or occupations are

   _____ courses.

3. Your area of specialization in school is your

   _____ .

4. Activities which are not part of the required course of study are

   _____ activities.

5. Armed forces which are not on active duty but are called in an

   emergency are _____ .

Understanding
Words

Which statement is a good example of the meaning of the vocabulary word? Circle A or B.

1. affirm
   A. "That statement is true."
   B. "Is that answer correct?"

2. convict
   A. "As the presiding judge in this case, I declare that the jury has found this man guilty of the crime of armed robbery."
   B. "As the arresting officer, I think this man is guilty of robbing a liquor store, and his trial is set for two weeks from today."

3. authorize
   A. "Please send us a copy of your birth certificate as soon as possible, in order that we may process your application."
   B. "You have my permission to sign my name and speak for me in all matters pertaining to this contract."

4. disclose
   A. "I've been a member of many organizations in my lifetime."
   B. "I admit that in 1954 I belonged to an organization called Americans for Democratic Action."

The present perfect tense is used to describe an action that began in the past and is still true in the present. Look at the following sentence.

> I have lived in this city for three years.
> (I moved to this city three years ago, and
> *I am still living here.*)

It is different from the past tense, which expresses a completed action.

> I lived in my native city until 1978.
> (I left my native city in 1978, and
> *I am not living there now.*)

To form the present perfect tense use *has* or *have* plus the past participle of the main verb. Look at the following sentences.

I	*have*	*been*	here *for* five years.
She	*has*	*seen*	the movie three times.
We	*have*	*lived*	here all our lives.
They	*have*	*worked*	here *since* 1975.

For and *since* are often used with the present perfect tense.
For indicates a *period* of time:

> *for three years*
> *for an hour*
> *for two days*

Since indicates a *point* in time when the action began:

> *since 1980*
> *since two o'clock*
> *since yesterday*

Ever and *never* are also used frequently with the present perfect. These words are used in statements and questions about your entire life experience. Look at the following sentences.

Have you *ever* flown in a helicopter?
No, I *never* have.
She has *never* visited South America.

Answer the following questions, which are sometimes asked on job application forms.

1. Have you ever been arrested? _____

2. Have you ever been convicted of a violation of the law? _____

3. Have you ever applied for unemployment? _____

4. Have you been to an employment agency before? _____

5. Have you ever served in the military (armed forces)? _____

6. Have you ever received a decoration (been decorated)? _____

7. Have you ever sustained a serious injury? _____

8. Have you ever had the measles? mumps? chicken pox? Other diseases? _____

Choose a partner and ask each other questions with "Have you ever . . . ? Use the following verb phrases.

paint a picture	miss a train
type a letter	see Niagara Falls
rent a car	eat Indian food
drive a truck	wear a tuxedo

Say It This Way

From the list below, choose an idiom that has the same meaning as the underlined phrase, and rewrite the complete sentence.

to look something over
to be in the same boat

to get through
to fill (it) out
to make oneself comfortable

1. Please <u>read</u> this report before the meeting.

   _____

   _____

2. "Our company is laying off many people; you and I are in <u>a</u> <u>similar situation</u>."

   _____

   _____

3. He sat down at a table and <u>completed</u> the application.

   _____

   _____

4. "I'm afraid we'll never <u>survive</u> this experience."

   _____

   _____

5. He took off his coat, sat down and <u>relaxed</u>.

   _____

   _____

Getting the Facts: Applications and Forms

Applications often seem to be long, detailed, and **overwhelming** at first glance. It is best to **concentrate** on one section at a time, and to follow instructions carefully.

First, you will be asked for your name, address, telephone number, and social security number. Always have this information with you. Be sure you know your zip code and the area code of your telephone number.

Some employment applications ask for more personal information than others. **Legally**, for purposes of employment you are not required to answer questions about your age, marital status, number of children, and **ethnic** or religious group. If you feel that any of this information will **prevent** you from getting the job, do not answer questions about it. However, *not* answering questions may also be a **disadvantage**.

Employers who have more than fifteen employees must observe the Civil Rights Act of 1964, which says that an employer cannot **discriminate** against anyone because of color, sex, religion, race, or place of birth. In their Help Wanted ads, these employers often state that their company is "an equal opportunity employer."

An employment application will usually require information about your education, military service, if any, work history, and job interest. Under work history, you will be asked to put both employer and supervisor. The employer is the company, agency, or individual who paid your salary. The supervisor is the person you worked under—your immediate boss. Frequently you will be asked your reason for leaving each job. It is better not to mention any personal **conflict**, to say you couldn't **get along with** your supervisor or other employees, or to simply write "personal reasons." It is better to state that you left for professional or financial **advancement**, a more **challenging** or **stimulating** job, or some other positive reason.

On an application you will frequently be asked for personal references. People who know you well should be asked to comment positively about your personality and ability. These people should not be employers or relatives. Seek out individuals who will impress a prospective employer, such as business people, bankers, doctors, teachers, or members of the clergy; and be sure to ask their permission before using their names on an application.

At the end of an application there is usually a place for the date and your signature. Do not print your name: a signature must be written in script. There is frequently an affidavit, which is a statement **certifying** that the information you have given is true. There may also be a statement from the employer or agency, which you should read carefully before you sign the application.

Always read carefully an application for a private employment agency. Be sure you understand clearly what fees you may be responsible for. Sometimes an agency sends people for jobs where the employer does not pay the fee. In that case the applicant must pay it, even if he or she thought it was a **fee-paid position**.

overwhelming	appearing impossible to do
(to) **concentrate**	(to) put all one's thoughts, attention, or effort on something
legally	required by law
ethnic	of a racial or cultural group
(to) **prevent**	(to) stop from happening
disadvantage	unfavorable circumstance
(to) **discriminate**	(to) give unfair treatment to a person
conflict	disagreement; struggle
(to) **get along with**	(to) have a good working relationship with
advancement	the act of moving ahead; success; promotion
(something that is) **challenging**	(something that) tests one's ability
(something that is) **stimulating**	(something that) increases one's interest
(to) **certify**	(to) state as true or accurate
fee-paid position	a job where the employer pays an employment agency's fee for finding an employee

What's It All About?

Answer the following questions with your teacher or in writing on a separate sheet of paper.

1. What kinds of questions are you not legally required to answer on an employment application?
2. What employers must observe the Civil Rights Act of 1964?
3. What are three appropriate answers for the question "Reason for leaving your present or previous job"?

4. What is a signature? An affidavit?
5. What is a fee-paid position?
6. What kinds of people should you give as character references?

Can We Talk?

Discuss the following question with a partner, in small groups, or in a large group with your teacher.

Do you think it would affect your chances of getting a job if you did not answer questions about marital status, date of birth, religion, race, and number of children? Why?

Putting It to Work

Read the *Guide to Following Instructions on a Form*, and then fill out the application on pages 130–31. For practice, also fill out the Employee Withholding form.

Guide to Following Instructions on a Form

Read the sample instructions given, and the examples of each one.

Instructions	*How to Do It*
Check one	✓yes no
Circle your answer	1 2 ③ 4 5 6
Underline your response	temporary or <u>permanent</u>
Place an X in the blank (notice if the blank is before or after the number.)	X̲ 1 ___ 2 ___ 3 1 ___ 2 X̲ 3 ___
Write, do not print	_ali_____
Please print	ALI_____
Do not write in this space	_____

If the form does not tell you whether to check, circle, underline, or place an X, follow these rules:

If there is a small line or box or circle, use a *check* or an X.

Languages you speak: English____, French____, Spanish____

Other____

If there is no line, box, or circle, you may either circle or underline.

Expected weekly wage: $100 $150 $200 $250

                            $100 $150   <u>$200</u> $250

If the form does not tell you whether to write or print, choose the one you can do the best. Be neat, write large enough, and have the letters rest on the lines.

Write dates in the order: month/day/year.
Abbreviate dates like this:
May 10, 1970:   05/10/70
January 12, 1982: 01/12/82

If it is necessary to explain an answer, write the explanation in the appropriate space.

Were you absent more than 5 days last year?

Yes____ No____

If yes, explain_____

APPLICATION FOR EMPLOYMENT

EQUAL OPPORTUNITY EMPLOYER M/F

PERSONAL INFORMATION   PLEASE PRINT

Date _____   Social Security No. _____

Name _____
          Last   First   Middle

Present Address _____
                    Street   City   State   Zip

Permanent Address _____
                      Street   City   State   Zip

Phone No._____ Height_____ Weight_____ Sex_____

Date of   U.S. Citizen or   Have You Ever Been
Birth_____ Alien Resident_____ Convicted of a Crime?_____

If Related to Anyone in Our Employ
State Name and Department _____

Referred by _____

EMPLOYMENT DESIRED

Position _____ Date You Can Start _____ Salary Desired _____

Are You Employed Now? _____ If So May We Inquire of Your Present Employer? _____

Have You Ever Applied to This
Company Before? _____ Where _____ When _____

EDUCATION

	School Name and Location	Years Attended	Date Graduated	Subjects Studied
Grammar School				
High School				ACAD. COMM. VOC.
College				MAJOR MINOR
Trade, Business or Correspondence School				

Subjects of Special Study or Research Work _____

What Foreign Languages Do You Speak Fluently? _____

Read _____   Write _____

Activities Other Than Religious
(Civic, Athletic, Etc.) _____

MILITARY

Years of Active Service_____ Decorations Received_____

FORMER EMPLOYERS

List Below Last Four Employers, Starting With Most Recent

Date Month and Year	Full Name and Address of Employer	Salary	Position	Reasons for Leaving
From				
To				
From				
To				
From				
To				
From				
To				

REFERENCES: Give Below the Names of Three Persons Not Related to You, Whom You Have Known At Least One Year.

	Name	Address	Business	Years Acquainted
1.				
2.				
3.				

PHYSICAL RECORD

List Any Physical Defects

Were You Ever Injured? Give Details

Have You Any Defects in Hearing? In Vision? In Speech?

In Case of Emergency Notify

Name Address Phone No.

I authorize investigation of all statements contained in this application. I understand that misrepresentation or omission of facts called for is cause for dismissal. Further, I understand and agree that my employment is for no definite period and may, regardless of the date of payment of my wages and salary, be terminated at any time without any previous notice.

Date Signature

DO NOT WRITE BELOW THIS LINE

Interviewed by Date

REMARKS:

Discrimination because of age, race, creed, color, or sex is prohibited by law. New York City law prohibits discrimination based on physical handicaps.

Form **W-4** (Rev. January 1985)	Department of the Treasury—Internal Revenue Service **Employee's Withholding Allowance Certificate**	OMB No. 1545-0010 Expires: 11-30-87

1 Type or print your full name

2 Your social security number

Home address (number and street or rural route)

City or town, State, and ZIP code

3 Marital Status .
- ☐ Single ☐ Married
- ☐ Married, but withhold at higher Single rate

Note: If married, but legally separated, or spouse is a nonresident alien, check the Single box.

4 Total number of allowances you are claiming (from line F of the worksheet on page 2) . . . .

5 Additional amount, if any, you want deducted from each pay . . . . $

6 I claim exemption from withholding because (see instructions and check boxes below that apply):

a ☐ Last year I did not owe any Federal income tax and had a right to a full refund of **ALL** income tax withheld, **AND**

b ☐ This year I do not expect to owe any Federal income tax and expect to have a right to a full refund of **ALL** income tax withheld. If both a and b apply, enter the year effective and "EXEMPT" here . . . ▶ Year

c If you entered "EXEMPT" on line 6b, are you a full-time student? . . . . ☐Yes ☐No

Under penalties of perjury, I certify that I am entitled to the number of withholding allowances claimed on this certificate, or if claiming exemption from withholding, that I am entitled to claim the exempt status.

Employee's signature ▶   Date ▶   , 19

7 Employer's name and address **(Employer: Complete 7, 8, and 9 only if sending to IRS)**

8 Office code

9 Employer identification number

Courtesy U.S. Government Printing Office.

9

INTERVIEW BEHAVIOR, VERBAL: SAMUEL'S STORY

Henry Wade:	Mr. Spacek? I'm Henry Wade. (He <u>extends</u> his hand)
Samuel:	How do you do? (They shake hands)
Henry Wade:	Please have a seat.
Samuel:	Thank you.
Henry Wade:	Do you have a résumé with you?
Samuel:	Yes, of course. (Samuel hands it to Mr. Wade)
Henry Wade:	(Reading) How do you pronounce your name?
Samuel:	Spah-chek.
Henry Wade:	I see, Mr. Spacek. (He looks at résumé <u>briefly</u>.) Why don't you tell me a little about yourself.
Samuel:	Well, in Prague I was the chief engineer of a construction <u>enterprise</u> for five years. I was responsible for testing the quality of prefabricated building materials.
Henry Wade:	Why do you want to work for this company?
Samuel:	I know that you are working with a new process for <u>stress</u> analysis, and I have many years of experience in this field. I could be very useful to your company.
Henry Wade:	Have you had any American experience?
Samuel:	Not in my <u>field</u>. I had a job as security guard for two months, but I had some trouble and I lost that job.
Henry Wade:	What kind of trouble?
Samuel:	Oh, I got sick with <u>hepatitis</u> and couldn't work for two months, so they <u>laid me off</u>.
Henry Wade:	(<u>sympathetically</u>) That's too bad.

134

Samuel:	Yes, and it was at a bad time. My wife was pregnant, and then we had no medical insurance for the hospital. I have an <u>enormous</u> hospital bill I must pay. You know, in my country we don't have such big medical expenses. It was all taken care of by the government.
Henry Wade:	Oh, really? Then this must be a big change for you.
Samuel:	Yes, it is. And you know, just yesterday my son had an accident with his bicycle and <u>knocked out</u> one of his teeth.
Henry Wade:	I'm sorry to hear that.
Samuel:	Yes, it's difficult. Does your company have medical insurance?
Henry Wade:	Yes, we do have a good <u>benefits package</u>. But it's too early to talk about that. Tell me more about your background. Where were you educated?
Samuel:	I attended the University of Prague and graduated with a degree in mechanical engineering. For twenty years I worked in site building for heavy industry. Then I worked for a manufacturing <u>firm</u> and was in charge of <u>quality control</u> for the stress factor on load bearing construction material.
Henry Wade:	Was that your last job before leaving your country?
Samuel:	Yes, unfortunately that plant was destroyed by fire.
Henry Wade:	You certainly have good experience. But you seem to have had a run of bad luck.
Samuel:	Yes, I know what you mean. And since I came to America, it's been one thing after another. It's not easy at my age.
Henry Wade:	Oh, how old are you, Mr. Spacek?
Samuel:	I'm fifty-three.
Henry Wade:	You don't look it. When you mentioned that you recently had a baby . . .
Samuel:	Yes, (smiling) my wife is <u>quite a bit</u> younger than I am—it's my second marriage. I have two grown children still in Czechoslovakia.
Henry Wade:	Mmmmmmn. Tell me, with your excellent background, why couldn't you find a better position than security guard?
Samuel:	Well, I looked for a job for two weeks, and I just

couldn't <u>afford</u> to stay out of work. I'm the kind of person <u>who</u> can't be without work.

Henry Wade: I see. Well, (looking at his watch) I have a few other <u>candidates</u> to interview today. You certainly seem to have the professional experience we're looking for. When we make a decision, we'll contact you.

Samuel: Thank you very much. I hope I didn't <u>bother</u> you with my problems, but you're such a sympathetic person—so easy to talk to.

Henry Wade: (smiling) Well, thank you, and good luck to you.

What Happened?

Write T if the sentence is true, F if it is false.

_____ 1. Samuel had his résumé with him.

_____ 2. The employer was not interested in Samuel's American experience.

_____ 3. Samuel lost his first job in the United States because of illness.

_____ 4. In Samuel's native country medical treatment was free.

_____ 5. Samuel is not worried about medical bills.

_____ 6. Samuel spoke about personal problems.

_____ 7. The employer thought Samuel was lucky.

_____ 8. Samuel was prepared for the interview.

Hidden Meanings

Think about the following questions carefully before discussing in class. If necessary, refer to the story.

1. Was Samuel's manner businesslike? Why or why not?

2. Did Samuel give any unnecessary information? If so, what was it?

3. Do you think the employer is impressed with Samuel's background?

4. Did Samuel give a positive impression?

5. What reason could Samuel have given for leaving his job as security guard?

6. What kind of preparation did Samuel do before the interview?

7. Do you think the employer will hire Samuel? Why or why not?

Finding the Definition

Circle the letter of the expression that has the same meaning as the underlined word or words.

1. The employer extended his hand to Samuel.
   a. held out
   b. shook
   c. raised

2. The employer seemed to listen to him sympathetically.
   a. politely
   b. with understanding
   c. usefully

3. Samuel had a job, but it was not in his field.
   a. district
   b. country
   c. specialization

4. He worked for a manufacturing firm.
   a. country
   b. company
   c. solid

5. The employer interviewed several candidates for the position.
   a. politicians
   b. applicants
   c. students

6. Samuel's wife is quite a bit younger than he is.
   a. a little
   b. a lot
   c. not very much

Finding the Word

Complete each statement using one of the vocabulary words underlined in the text.

1. To pronounce incorrectly is to _____.

2. A disease affecting the liver is _____.

3. Other words for a *business* are a _____ or an _____.

4. Checking and maintaining specific standards for a finished product is called _____ _____.

5. The total benefits offered by a company to its employees is called a _____ _____.

6. A word that means *very large* is _____.

7. To have enough money for something is to be able to _____ it.

Understanding Words

Which statement is a good example of the meaning of the vocabulary word? Circle A or B.

1. sympathetic
   A. "I'm so sorry to hear that the company laid you off."
   B. "Well, that's life. Don't feel so sorry for yourself."

2. brief
   A. "Do you like your job?" "Yes, I do."
   B. "Do you like your job?" "Oh the job is just the type of work I've been looking for. I love it."

3. bother
   A. "Could I borrow your newspaper if you are finished with it?"
   B. "Excuse me. Don't turn the page yet, because I'm reading the newspaper over your shoulder and I haven't finished that article."

In English there are many verbs that contain two or more words. Some of these verbs are separable, which means they can have a noun or pronoun object between the two words of the verb.

Look at the following sentences.

John *turned off* the lights.
John *turned* the lights *off*.
John *turned* them *off*.

If the object is a pronoun, it must appear in the middle. If the object is a noun, it can appear in the middle or at the end.

Rewrite the following sentences, and place a noun and then a pronoun between the two-word verb.

Example: Muhammad Ali *knocked out* the challenger.
Muhammad Ali *knocked*   the challenger *out*.
Muhammad Ali *knocked*   him   *out*.

1. The company *laid off* six employees.

   _____

   _____

2. The government *closed down* the factory.

   _____

   _____

3. I must leave early to *pick up* my daughter at school.

   _____

   _____

4. It happened two weeks ago. Why are you *bringing up* that point now?

   _____

   _____

5. I don't know what he looks like. Please *point out* the president to me.

_____

_____

6. We can't *put off* the meeting any longer.

_____

_____

7. Would you *look over* these reports, please?

_____

_____

8. I'd like to *think over* your offer.

_____

_____

9. I regret that we must *turn down* that applicant.

_____

_____

10. We shouldn't *pass up* this opportunity.

_____

_____

Say It This Way

From the list below, choose an idiom that has the same meaning as the underlined phrase, and rewrite the complete sentence.

(it's been) one thing after another
quite a bit
a run of (good or bad luck)

1. This report requires <u>a lot</u> of work.

_____

_____

2. It was just a series of unfortunate incidents: the fuses blew out, the president broke his leg, and then the speaker didn't arrive.

_____

_____

_____

3. From what you have been telling me, it appears you have had an uninterrupted period of trouble.

_____

_____

_____

Getting the Facts: The Employment Interview

In a country where jobs are not guaranteed and employers interview several people for each job, the job interview has become a science. This science can be learned, but there is an important point to remember: Not everyone is successful on a first interview. A successful interview takes plenty of practice.

The key to any successful interview is preparation. There are several things to think about before you go on an interview:

What do you know about the company?
What skills do you have that specifically fit the job?
What questions do you expect the interviewer to ask you?
What questions should you ask the interviewer?

When you go on an interview, you are at an important point in the job search. *The interviewer is interested in you.* You may be the person he or she is looking for. But you must prove that you understand the company's needs and that you have the professional skills and personal attributes to do the job. *Be ready to speak confidently about yourself.* Before the interview, write down a detailed record of your accomplishments: the things you have done over the years, and problems you have **confronted** and solved. Then write down the ways in which your experience relates to the needs of the job. Practice saying these things *out loud*: reading them over is not enough.

If there are any factors against you, such as lack of certain skills or experience, be prepared to explain to the employer how you plan to overcome your **deficiencies**.

Here is a list of questions and comments an interviewer might ask you or say to you. Think about how you would respond to each one.

What can I do for you?
Tell me about yourself.
Why do you want to work here?
Why should we **hire** you?
Where would you like to be five years from now?
Why are you leaving your present job?
What salary are you looking for?
What is your minimum salary **requirement**?
Why haven't you gotten a job so far?
What are some of your biggest accomplishments?
What kind of manager do you think you'd make?
Can you work under **pressure**? Against **deadlines**?
Do you want to continue your education?
What is your greatest strength? Weakness?
Are you capable of making quick decisions?
What did you dislike about your **previous** job?
What interests you most about the job here?
How would you describe your personality?
What are your hobbies?
It seems you are overqualified for this job.
Do you think your English is good enough for this job?
Why did you come to this country?

When you answer a question during an interview, the word "yes" by itself is generally not enough. Give additional information that shows why "yes" is the correct answer.

Some interviewers are **aggressive** and will **fire** questions at you rapidly. Be ready to answer them. Keep in mind that employers may purposely make you feel uncomfortable because they want to see your reactions under stressful conditions. Other interviewers are mostly **passive**, or "**low-key**," and want you to do the talking. That is why you must be prepared to both listen and speak.

Some non-native adults feel that listening is easier than speaking; they are nervous that at an interview they will not express

142

themselves well. Remember that mistakes in language are only a part of the general impression you make in a job interview. Never say "My English is not so good." Instead, say something positive about how you are taking courses and constantly improving your language skills.

Keep in mind that the employer is not only considering the way you speak, but is looking at you **as a whole**. Don't **underestimate** the importance of qualities other than job skills, which you can bring to the job: maturity and life experience, responsibility, **willingness** to learn new things, willingness to work hard, ability to **adapt** to difficult situations, **initiative**, pride in your work, **dependability**, **creativity**, or the ability to work in an organized way. These are qualities to emphasize.

The interviewer may ask you if you have any questions about the job. The following are questions you may ask if the interviewer has not already given you the information.

What skills are required for the job?
What are the specific duties and responsibilities of the job?
What kind of personality works well in this job?
What would my hours be? What is the work schedule?
What are my opportunities for advancement?

Most experts agree that you should not ask about salary and benefits unless you are reasonably sure the employer is seriously **considering** hiring you. If you are sure, you may ask:

What is the salary for the job?
What benefits does your company offer?

When you leave an interview, thank the interviewer for his or her time and consideration. Ask when you will be notified of the company's decision. Most businesses will inform you within two weeks. If you have not received an answer after a reasonable amount of time, follow up with a letter or telephone call.

Of course, you may decide on the basis of your interview that you do not want the job. If you are offered the job, ask for a day or two to consider the offer and then inform the interviewer what you have decided. Never accept a job and then fail to **show up**. Keep in mind that employers in the same field often know each other. Unprofessional **behavior** with one employer could cause you trouble with another employer.

If you are called back for a second interview for a job that you want, congratulations. This means that you are being seriously considered for the job.

If you don't get the job, don't be **insulted**, and don't be discouraged. It is not unusual to go through many interviews before getting a job. It may take several interviews to get the job you really want.

Remember that as an applicant you have the right to ask the interviewer questions. Listen carefully to what the interviewer is saying, because he or she could be giving you valuable information. Take your time and think carefully about how you feel about that information.

Whether English is a person's second language or native language, job-hunting can be a difficult and frustrating process. Practice and preparation will help to make it easier and more interesting.

Glossed Words

(to) **confront**	(to) stand face to face with
deficiency	lack of a quality or attribute
(to) **hire**	(to) employ
requirement	necessity; need
pressure	the burden of physical or mental stress
deadline	time limit before or by which something must be completed
previous	prior; earlier; former
aggressive	very forceful; attacking
(to) **fire** (questions) at	(to) ask questions very quickly with force
passive	inactive
low-key	not talking much; quiet
as a whole	in total
(to) **underestimate**	(to) put too low a value on something

144

willingness	readiness
(to) **adapt**	(to) adjust to a situation
initiative	ability to undertake something on one's own
dependability	trustworthiness; reliability
creativity	quality of being able to produce original work or ideas
(to) **consider**	(to) think about
(to) **show up**	(to) arrive; make an appearance
behavior	manner of one's conduct
(to) **insult**	(to) offend

What's It All About?

Answer the following questions with your teacher or in writing on a separate sheet of paper.

1. What must you be ready to do before you walk into an interview?

2. What could you say when asked about your ability to speak English?

3. What other things do you bring to the employer besides job skills?

4. What shouldn't you discuss at a first interview?

5. What should you do if you have not received an answer from an employer within a reasonable time?

Can We Talk?

Discuss the following questions with a partner, in small groups, or in a large group with your teacher.

1. What would be the most difficult question for you to answer that might be asked on a job interview?

2. How would you respond to the question, "Tell me about yourself"? (Suggestion: In *one to two minutes* briefly discuss your early years, education, past experience, and your recent experience.)

Putting It to Work

With a partner, practice the following sentences orally.

From _____ to _____ I attended _____

_____ .

I graduated from _____ in _____ .

I received a _____ from _____ in

_____ .

From _____ to _____ I worked as a _____

_____ at _____ .

My responsibilities there were _____ .

I was responsible for _____ .

I was in the army from _____ to _____ . In the army I

served as a _____ .

English is not my native language, but I'm studying and improving every day.

I didn't quite understand you. Could you repeat the question, please?

I have never worked with that process (machine, equipment) but I worked with something very similar, and I am sure I will catch on quickly.

I have the experience you are looking for. (Give examples to prove it.)

I get along very well with other people. (Give examples to prove it.)

I am well qualified to complete this project. (Give examples to prove it.)

If I am employed by your company, you can be sure of my loyalty and responsibility.

I can work under stress. It does not bother me. (Give examples to prove it.)

I have the ambition to get ahead in your organization if I am given the opportunity.

Thank you very much, Mr. (Ms.)_____ . I appreciate your taking the time to talk with me.

Read the following job interview and analyze it by answering the questions that follow.

Arthur is a senior in high school. He is looking for a summer job at a fast-food restaurant. American teenagers frequently work after the age of sixteen, at part-time jobs after school, on weekends, and full- or part-time jobs during the summer. They work in restaurants, movie theaters, supermarkets, gas stations, stores, and so on.

This is Arthur's first job interview. You will see that he still has a lot to learn.

Manager:	Hello.
Arthur:	Hello.
Manager:	Why do you want this job?
Arthur:	I need the money.
Manager:	Do you work well under pressure?
Arthur:	Yes, I've had experience at the Town Theater working at the candy counter. One afternoon I served over five hundred people.
Manager:	Are you still working there?
Arthur:	No.
Manager:	Why did you leave that job?
Arthur:	I left because I didn't get along with the boss.
Manager:	Did you give them two weeks' notice?
Arthur:	Well, no, actually I was fired. I sort of left by mutual consent.
Manager:	Could I call them for a recommendation?
Arthur:	You could, but you'd better not because I don't think she would give me a good one.

Manager:	Why not?
Arthur:	Well, I did my work well, but we didn't get along.
Manager:	What didn't you like about that job?
Arthur:	When I was taking tickets at the door, I didn't like standing in one place for four or five hours.
Manager:	Are you going away in September?
Arthur:	Yes, I'm going to college.
Manager:	O.K. If you're hired, we'll call you in about a week.
Arthur:	If you don't call me, should I come down?
Manager:	No, don't bother.
Arthur:	Well, thank you very much. Goodbye.
Manager:	Goodbye.

Discuss the following questions in small groups, or in a large group, analyzing Arthur's interview.

1. What were some of the good and bad things in the interview?

2. How else could Arthur have answered the following questions?
   a. Why do you want this job?
   b. Why did you leave that job?
   c. Did you give two weeks' notice?
   d. Could I call them for a recommendation?
   e. What didn't you like about your other job?
   f. Are you going away in September?

Role-plays

For each role-play one person plays the person described in the left column, who is looking for a job. The other person plays the person described in the right column, who is an employer. Act out a job interview between the two people. After the interview, let the class decide if the applicant will get the job.

Person being interviewed	*Interviewer*
1. This woman is in her mid 40s. She was a music teacher in her native country. She worked in a school	This woman is in her mid 30's, and is the owner of a small, fashionable boutique. She is energetic, nervous, and busi-

with hundreds of children. She has never sold before, but she does not like clerical work, and would like to get into sales. She has good taste, and enjoys being well-dressed.

nesslike. She doesn't like to waste time. She needs a salesperson.

2. This woman is in her mid 30s. In her native country she was an economist. She has just completed a course in a business school, has bookkeeping skills, and can do light typing at about thirty-five words per minute.

This man is the owner of a small import-export company. Many of his clients speak the applicant's native language. He is a sympathetic person, but wants a bookkeeper who will give him a good day's work.

3. This man is a college student, age 20, who wants to work over the summer vacation. He wants a job that requires a lot of physical work.

This man is 52, very strong, big, and serious. He owns a construction company and sometimes employs summer workers for heavy jobs like pouring cement, etc.

Do you have a "dream job?" What job would you want if you could have any job in the world? Act out an interview for your dream job with another student in the class. Before beginning the interview make sure your partner understands what the job is and the qualifications for it.

10

INTERVIEW BEHAVIOR, NONVERBAL: GISELA'S STORY

"Please come in, Ms. Infante, and have a seat," said Ms. Goodman as she hurried to her desk to pick up the phone. Gisela realized that there were several places in the office where she could sit, and for the moment she didn't know which seat would be appropriate. Should she take the chair directly in front of the desk or the one to the side of the desk? Or perhaps it would be more comfortable for her to sit on the couch against the wall. She couldn't just stand there, so she finally decided to sit in front of the desk. Somehow, she did not feel that she had made the wisest choice, since the desk created a barrier between her and the interviewer.

Ms. Goodman was busy talking on the phone. "Good," thought Gisela. That would give her time to look around the office and think of some comment she might make at the beginning of the interview. It would break the ice before getting down to business. There were beautiful photographs on the wall, but Gisela also noticed that Ms. Goodman's desk was completely cluttered with papers and drawings. Gisela liked everything to have a place, and this looked very disorganized to her.

By this time, fifteen minutes had passed and Ms. Goodman was still talking on the phone. Gisela felt uncomfortable, as if she were taking valuable time from Ms. Goodman's busy day. Finally the phone call ended, and Ms. Goodman apologized for taking so long. She offered Gisela a cup of coffee, which Gisela politely declined, not knowing whether that was the right thing to do.

Ms. Goodman then began the interview, which lasted about twenty-five minutes. Gisela was never more unsure of anything in her life. Ms. Goodman had asked her some very difficult questions, which Gisela hoped she had answered well. However, there were still many confusing aspects to the meeting.

For one thing, Ms. Goodman's <u>mode</u> of dress made Gisela uncomfortable. Gisela thought Ms. Goodman looked unusual in her jeans and boots, which seemed more like something to wear on a day off rather than on a workday. "What kind of <u>executive</u> is this?" thought Gisela. She began to have some doubts about her own <u>outfit</u>. Was she dressed too <u>conservatively</u> in her dark tailored suit? And did she really want to work for this person?

Gisela felt as though she had entered a world she didn't understand. There were so many <u>conflicting</u> messages.

What Happened?

Answer the following questions.

1. Where did Gisela decide to sit?

_____

2. How long did the interviewer keep Gisela waiting?

_____

3. Did Gisela accept a cup of coffee from the interviewer?

_____

4. How long was the interview?

_____

5. Why was Gisela puzzled about the interviewer's style of dress?

_____

6. What made Gisela uncomfortable?

_____

Hidden Meanings

Think about the following questions carefully before discussing in class. If necessary, refer to the story.

1. What conflicting messages did Gisela receive?
2. Why was she worried about where to sit?

3. Why did the cluttered desk disturb her?

4. Why was she confused about the interview?

5. Why did she begin to worry about how she was dressed?

Finding the Definition

Circle the letter of the expression that has the same meaning as the underlined word or words.

1. Gisela did not feel that she had made the <u>wisest</u> choice.
   a. most interesting
   b. smartest
   c. nearest

2. The desk created a <u>barrier</u> between them.
   a. a path
   b. a wall
   c. a bridge

3. She looks so casual. She isn't dressed like an <u>executive</u>.
   a. efficient person
   b. secretary
   c. person with administrative authority

4. Jane's office is so small that she has no place for anything—the desk is always <u>cluttered</u>.
   a. orderly
   b. messy
   c. organized

5. Vogue Magazine shows the current <u>modes</u> of fashion.
   a. illustrations
   b. styles
   c. models

6. The party <u>lasted</u> until 3:00 A.M.
   a. stopped
   b. most recent
   c. continued

Match the words in Column A with the antonym in Column B.

Column A	Column B
1. ____ appropriate	a. clear
2. ____ wise	b. unsuitable
3. ____ cluttered	c. peace
4. ____ decline	d. confident
5. ____ unsure	e. foolish
6. ____ conflict	f. accept
7. ____ conservative	g. revolutionary
8. ____ confusing	h. neat

Which statement is a good example of the meaning of the vocabulary word? Circle A or B.

1. <u>appropriate</u>
   A. "This is exactly the right dress for this party."
   B. "Oh, dear, I'm the only woman in this room wearing an evening gown. Everyone else is dressed informally."

2. <u>disorganized</u>
   A. "I have so many things to do I don't know what to do first; I'll never be finished."
   B. "I'm making a list of everything I have to do, and I'll finish one thing at a time."

3. <u>decline</u>
   A. "Thank you, I'd love some tea."
   B. "I won't eat anything, thank you—I've just had lunch."

4. <u>unsure</u>
   A. "I'm positive that she liked me."
   B. "Maybe I said the wrong thing. I didn't really understand her question."

5. conflicting
   A. "Wait a minute—we're going to dinner with your boss on Friday at 8:00, but this letter from Mother asks us to meet her at the airport on Friday at 7:45!"
   B. "No problem. We can see Mary in the afternoon and still have time to go to the concert in the evening."

6. break the ice
   A. "Here is my résumé. What would you like to know about me?"
   B. "You have such a beautiful view from your window. It must be a pleasure to work here."

Learning through Practice: Indirect Commands and Requests

Orders or commands are expressed in indirect speech by the use of an infinitive.

direct: She said to me, "Be quiet."
indirect: She told me to be quiet.

direct: John said to me, "Don't smoke on the subway."
indirect: John told me not to smoke on the subway.

Change these sentences to the indirect speech form.

1. They said to me, "Come back later."

   _____

2. The interviewer said to her, "Think about it."

   _____

3. I said to him, "Leave me alone."

   _____

4. The teacher said to them, "Don't be late."

   _____

5. The doctor said to me, "Make an appointment with my secretary."

   _____

6. My mother said to me, "Don't open the door for anybody."

_____

Polite requests: If the word <u>please</u> is used in direct speech, we use <u>ask</u> instead of <u>tell</u> in indirect speech.

    direct: She said to me, "Please come in."
indirect: <u>She asked me to come in.</u>
    direct: I said to my daughter, "Please don't go out."
indirect: <u>I asked my daughter not to go out.</u>

7. Mrs. Jones said to her husband, "Please pass the salt."

_____

8. The interviewer said to Martina, "Please sit down."

_____

9. My husband said to me, "Please don't drive so fast."

_____

10. The secretary said to Troy, "Please follow me."

_____

Say It This Way

Match each idiom in Column A with its definition in Column B.

Column A	Column B
a. to take long	____ to be properly located
b. to break the ice	____ to begin to talk seriously
c. to have a seat	____ to use a lot of time
d. to get down to business	____ to sit down
e. to have a place	____ to create a comfortable feeling at the beginning of a conversation

Getting the Facts: Nonverbal Communication During an Interview

What we do is often more important than what we say. The way we dress, the way we walk, the way we sit and where we sit, the way we look or don't look at other people, how early or late we are—these things, which are all elements of **nonverbal** *communication,* are responsible for over 60 percent of the **impression** we make on other people.

Nonverbal communication exists in every culture. To be able to communicate with others effectively, a newcomer to any country must learn that culture's system of nonverbal communication. For example, in the United States it is important to give a **firm handshake** to an interviewer; it shows confidence and **straightforwardness.** You should always make eye contact with the interviewer while either of you are speaking. Many Americans feel that people who do not look at them while either listening or talking, or who **shift** their eyes away, are trying to hide something.

The nonverbal communication in an interview really begins before the interview, with your arrival. Come alone to the interview. If you bring someone else to interpret for you or give you "moral support," you **convey** a lack of confidence in your ability to stand on your own. Never arrive late. It is best to arrive five or ten minutes early so that you have time to **compose** yourself and appear poised for the interview.

First impressions are created in a few seconds. Make sure you are neat, clean, and **well groomed,** not too **dressed up** and not too **sporty**. Don't wear flashy jewelry, heavy make-up, or too much cologne or perfume. Nothing should distract the interviewer from you or your qualifications. For any professional job, a suit, shirt, and tie for a man and a suit with a skirt and a simple pastel blouse for a woman will make the best impression. Good colors for interview clothes are brown, black, grey, blue, and beige. Matching suits are the most effective; the more tailored and **conservative** you look, the better. Of course, style of dress may **vary**, depending upon what type of job you are being interviewed for. Some suggest that, if possible, you visit the company before going on the interview to get a better idea of the company's dress code.

During an interview, it's important to be aware of the distance between you and the interviewer. **Research** shows that the best distance between people in business conversations is between

158

twenty-one and thirty-six inches. If you are closer than that, an American will feel that you are invading his or her "personal space," will feel uncomfortable, and will begin to **back away**. If you are farther than thirty-six inches, you will not be able to speak in a normal, relaxed tone of voice. For an interview, the seat that provides the most comfortable speaking distance, if the interviewer is behind the desk, is the chair at the side of the desk.

Your **posture** during an interview is also important. Whether you are sitting or standing, your posture communicates to the interviewer whether you are an interested, **alert, energetic** person or a tired, unsure, nervous person. This is called *body language*. The interviewer's body language can also communicate information to you. For example, if he or she glances at the clock, says "uh-huh" too much, plays with a paper clip, or **fidgets** in the chair, you may be talking too much. Then, it would be time to "**give the floor back**" to the interviewer. The interviewer will also give you certain nonverbal signals when the interview is over, such as looking at his or her watch, making a phone call, calling the secretary, or even standing up.

Glossed Words

nonverbal	not using words
impression	what someone thinks about another
firm	strong; solid
handshake	taking another's hand in greeting
straightforward	direct
(to) **shift**	(to) change position
(to) **convey**	(to) communicate
(to) **compose**	(to) calm oneself
well groomed	carefully dressed; very neat
dressed up	wearing special clothing
sporty	informal clothing
(to) **distract**	(to) take attention away

conservative	traditional; moderate
(to) **vary**	(to) be different; change form
research	study or investigation of a subject
(to) **back away**	(to) move backwards
posture	position of the body
alert	lively; awake
energetic	showing energy; active
(to) **fidget**	(to) move nervously
(to) **"give the floor back"**	(to) allow the other person to speak

What's It All About?

Answer the following questions with your teacher or in writing on a separate sheet of paper.

1. What is nonverbal communication?

2. Why is it important to understand the system of nonverbal communication in the country where you are living?

3. Why is a firm handshake important?

4. Why is it important to make eye contact with an interviewer?

5. What is meant by body language? Give an example.

6. What are some conservative colors for business clothes?

Can We Talk?

Discuss the following questions with a partner, in small groups, or in a large group with your teacher.

1. How important is it that you sit in the right place during an interview?

2. In your native country, is the use of space different from the use of space in the United States? In your country, how close do people stand when they speak?

3. How does nonverbal communication differ in your native culture in terms of physical contact, eye contact, dress, gestures (beckoning, waving, counting on fingers, striking a match, etc. What corresponds to the American "thumbs down, thumbs up"?), facial expressions, and time?

Putting It to Work

1. What does the body language in the four drawings below tell us?

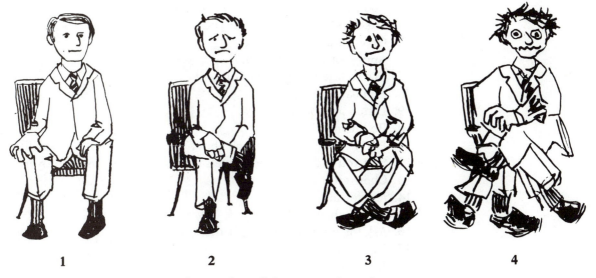

| 1 | 2 | 3 | 4 |

Next to each adjective, write the number of the appropriate picture.

____worried   ____confident
____interested   ____frantic
____nervous   ____unsure
____tired   ____"bananas"
____alert   ____exhausted

2. You are working for a filmmaker, and you have been asked to create the costumes for the next movie.

   In small groups, discuss what the actors and actresses playing these roles should wear:

   a model   an accountant
   a teacher   a mechanic

a banker   a salesperson
an artist   a bank teller
a secretary   a flight attendant

How to Handle the Interview

Listed below are some things that can "make or break" a job interview. *Put an X next to the ones which you feel might help you get a job.* There are sixteen correct answers.

1. Say you really need the job.
2. Learn about the company first.
3. Look at the person interviewing you.
4. Take another person with you.
5. Give a weak handshake.
6. Apply for a specific job.
7. Arrive late for the appointment.
8. Be neat and clean.
9. Listen and be polite.
10. Be businesslike.
11. Early in the interview ask about vacations and other benefits.
12. Say you didn't get along well with your previous employer.
13. Chew gum.
14. Ask for a cigarette.
15. Arrive ahead of time.
16. Ask for information about the job.
17. Dress conservatively.
18. Look interested and alert.
19. Think before answering questions.
20. Apologize for your English.
21. After the interview, thank the employer for his or her time.
22. Stare at the floor.
23. Have facts about your former jobs and your qualifications.
24. Talk about things that have nothing to do with the job.
25. Show eagerness to learn.
26. Discuss personal problems.
27. Bite your nails.
28. Emphasize your strong points.
29. Tell the employer how to run his or her business.
30. Show how your skills fit the employer's needs.

Compare your answers with those of your teacher.

11

ON-THE-JOB BEHAVIOR, ACTION: MARTHA, KIM, HORACE

Scene I: Martha

Martha was sitting at her desk, <u>wondering</u> how much longer she would have to work tonight in order to finish all her paperwork. She didn't want to <u>trust</u> just anyone with those lab reports. Her new job was too important. She knew that she was a little behind schedule with her assignments, but at least she could make sure the reports were done correctly if she did them herself.

Martha felt that the secretary who normally typed the reports for her made too many mistakes. Last month when she gave the secretary her report to type, <u>xerox</u>, <u>collate</u>, and <u>staple</u>, Martha ended up <u>redoing</u> the entire job herself.

She felt that she couldn't afford to lose this job. It had taken her too long to find it. Martha wanted all of her work to be perfect.

What Happened?

Answer the following question.

Why was Martha working late?

_____

Hidden Meanings

Think about the following question carefully before discussing in class. If necessary, refer to the story.

Why was Martha afraid she would lose her job if the secretary typed her reports?

The other day, Kim's coworker, Marty, had asked Kim to accompany him to talk to the boss about his plan for solving a problem in the office.

Marty knocked on the boss's door and walked into Bill Williams' office with Kim behind him. Mr. Williams said, "Well, Marty, Kim, what's up? Make yourselves comfortable. What can I do for you guys?"

Marty began by saying, "Well, Mr. Williams," but the boss interrupted him. "Don't be so formal," he said. "My name is Bill." Marty began talking about the office problem. As Marty was speaking, Bill Williams leaned back in his chair and put his feet up on the desk. He disagreed with Marty about certain things, but continued to discuss the proposed plan. Kim was a little confused by the informal way they were speaking, so he didn't say anything.

Finally, Bill Williams sat up, looked directly at Kim and Marty, changed his tone of voice and said, "Your idea is good, but according to company policy we have to follow certain steps in order to make this decision. If you give me your proposal in writing, I'll review it carefully, present it to the board, and I'll get back to you as soon as possible." He glanced at his watch.

Marty said he realized Bill must be very busy. He and Kim thanked him for his time and left the office.

Answer the following questions.

1. Why did Marty want to talk to the boss?

   _____

2. In what way was the boss informal?

   _____

3. What did the boss agree to do?

   _____

Hidden
Meanings

Think about the following questions carefully before discussing in class. If necessary, refer to the story.

1. Why was Kim confused about the employer's informal manner?

2. How did Marty know that the employer wanted to end the interview?

Scene III:
Horace

Horace had not expected to stay so long visiting his family in his native country. He had planned a two-week vacation, but it <u>ended up as</u> three-and-half weeks. First, his sister's husband died. Then, his father became <u>ill</u> and had to go to the hospital. Horace had to make some important decisions, and take care of many family matters, so he felt he had no choice but to stay the extra ten days. He knew he had <u>accumulated</u> a lot of sick days, so he was not worried about the extra time.

At last everything was settled, and Horace was ready to leave. When he got on the plane, he couldn't believe that he was finally <u>heading</u> home. After all the problems, he was almost looking forward to returning to work.

Arriving home from the airport, Horace sat down to relax and started <u>thumbing through</u> his mail. He was <u>amazed</u> to see how many bills and how much junk mail had accumulated while he was away. He noticed that one of the envelopes was a mailgram. Who could be sending him a mailgram? He hoped it wasn't from his family! He opened it and read:

```
To: Mr. Horace Perrelle        Date: 7/13/85

From: S & G International, Inc.


This is to notify you that since you were ex-
pected back at work on 7/6/85 and to date have
not returned or contacted any member of the
company we are taking your lack of contact as
your voluntary resignation from S & G Interna-
tional effective immediately.


Personnel Department

Paul Marx, Director
```

Answer the following questions.

1. Why did Horace stay so long visiting his family?

_____

2. Why did he feel it was not a problem to take the extra days?

_____

3. What had accumulated while he was away?

_____

4. What did Horace receive from his employer?

_____

Hidden
Meanings

Think about the following question carefully before discussing in class. If necessary, refer to the story.

Why didn't Horace inform his employer that he was staying on vacation longer than two weeks?

Finding
the Definition

Circle the letter of the expression that has the same meaning as the underlined word or words.

1. You must <u>redo</u> this report; it is full of mistakes.
   a. check over
   b. correct
   c. do again

2. Will you <u>accompany me</u> to the supermarket?
   a. come with me
   b. show me the way
   c. escort me

3. The plane was <u>heading for</u> Los Angeles.
   a. leaving
   b. moving in the direction of
   c. speeding toward

4. How many sick days have you <u>accumulated</u>?
   a. collected
   b. remaining
   c. all together, for the year

5. His father became <u>ill</u>, and needed help.
   a. poor
   b. angry
   c. sick

6. His decision to leave was <u>voluntary</u>; he was not asked to resign.
   a. temporary
   b. something he wanted to do
   c. compulsory

Complete each statement using one of the vocabulary words underlined in the text.

1. A letter that states that you are voluntarily leaving your job is a

   letter of _____ .

2. A person who works at the same place as you is your

   _____ .

3. To offer a plan for solving a problem is to make a

   _____ .

4. To begin speaking before someone else is finished speaking is to

   _____ that person.

5. To put printed or photocopied pages in the correct order is to

   _____ them.

6. A group of directors who are responsible for a corporation is a

   _____ of directors.

7. A guiding principle or rule is a _____ .

8. A rule or plan that goes into effect right away is

   _____   _____ .

Which statement is a good example of the meaning of the vocabulary word? Circle A or B.

1. proposal
   A. "I have written a letter to the President criticizing his economic policies."
   B. "I have written a description of my plan for starting a new English program in the evening."

2. wondering
   A. "What is the weather like in California? I am going there on vacation and I'm trying to decide what clothes to take."
   B. "I'm positive that it will rain today; look at those clouds."

3. amazed
   A. "Of course he won the first prize. It's not surprising. He's the best student in the school.
   B. "I am really surprised and impressed that you could finish so much work in one day."

4. trust
   A. "I can tell him anything, because I know that he won't say one word to anybody else."
   B. "I don't like that man. He always looks like he's hiding something."

5. according to
   A. "By the laws of our constitution, all persons of eighteen years and over may vote."
   B. "Contrary to your belief, in this office we work until five o'clock."

6. resignation
   A. "I would like to get into another profession."
   B. "I have decided to leave this company as of next Friday."

Learning through Practice: Future Conditions

A conditional sentence is a sentence containing two clauses:

(a) a *dependent clause beginning with if*
(b) a *main clause* that is the answer to, or the result of, the *if clause*

In the future conditional, the present tense is used in the *if clause* and the future tense in the main clause. This type of conditional sentence is called a *future possible condition* because it describes a simple situation that will take place in the future.

Notice that a *comma* is used only when the *if clause* comes *first*.

Give the correct form of the verb in parentheses.

Example: If he (work)__works__ hard, he (pass)__will pass__ his exam.

1. If it (rain)_____ tomorrow, we (stay)_____ home.

2. If you (no, write)_____ letters to your friends, they (no, write)_____ to you.

3. If you (no, call)_____ in when you are sick, your employer (be)_____ very annoyed.

The position of the two clauses may be reversed.

Example: You (make)__will make__ a lot of money if you (work)__work__ hard.

4. His English (improve) _____ if he (study)_____ .

5. We (go)_____ to the beach tomorrow if it (be)_____ nice.

Complete the following sentences using your own words.

1. We will make a profit if_____.

2. I will go out later if_____.

3. If you arrive late to an interview,_____.

4. I will call you if_____.

5. If a person is prepared before an interview,_____.

6. If a person drinks too much liquor,_____.

7. (to a child) If you don't clean up your room,_____.

8. (to a landlord) If you don't _____, _____.

9. We will miss the plane if_____.

10. I will give him your message if_____.

Say It This Way

Match the idioms in Column A with the definitions in Column B.

Column A	Column B
a. in order to	____to contact someone again
b. to thumb through	____to sit straight in the chair
c. according to	____to become
d. what's up?	____letters, reports, or forms to be written or read
e. to get back to someone	____for the purpose of
f. to sit up	____to look through quickly
g. to end up as	____what's happening; what's on your mind?
h. paperwork	____following; in agreement with

Getting the Facts: On-the-Job Behavior—the Written and Unwritten Rules

A popular old American song says, "My time is your time, your time is my time. . . ." This may be true in songs or romantic movies, but it is certainly not true in the American working world. Employers **regard** any time that you are paid for as their time, and time is money. Some office managers count hours and minutes as though they were gold coins.

Conflicts about the use of time can result in the loss of your job. It is therefore important to understand what your employer expects. Never change your working schedule—shift lunch hours, come in later, or leave earlier—without getting your supervisor's approval. Making such changes is **tampering** with time that is not really yours. If you must be late to work or absent, be sure to call your employer early in the morning. Take care of all personal business on your own time—before or after work, on lunch hours, or during holidays and annual leave days. Annual leave days include vacation days, sick days, personal days, and religious holidays. Sick leave is considered separately.

In order to know what is expected of you on your job, you need to know both the written and the **unwritten** rules. Written rules, such as the time to arrive and the time to leave, are clear, but unwritten rules about such things as the dress code and personal phone calls are less **obvious**. It is wise to communicate with your coworkers or your supervisor or employer and to keep your eyes and ears open to learn what is expected of you in situations that are not "spelled out."

What things are important to your immediate supervisor? Does he or she want you to contribute suggestions or just agree? Who do you call by his or her first name? What is the personality of the company? The type of business that a company does often decides its attitude toward employee behavior. One company may value teamwork and another may not. For example, a company that is involved in financial planning may require a more formal atmosphere and encourage people to work independently, while an advertising company or a company involved in fashion would want team effort between all departments. This would mean a great deal of interpersonal communication.

Unwritten rules are just as important as written rules. It is necessary to listen and observe to **determine** how you should act on your job.

Glossed Words

(to) **regard**	(to) consider; think about
(to) **tamper with**	(to) interfere with; change
unwritten	not recorded on paper; oral; traditional
obvious	standing out; noticeable
(to) **determine**	(to) decide

What's It All About?

Answer the following questions with your teacher or in writing on a separate sheet of paper.

1. What are some "written rules" of work?

2. What are some "unwritten rules" of work?

3. How does the employer regard the employee's paid time?

4. What are some reasons for losing a job?

5. What do we mean by the "personality" of a company?

Can We Talk?

Discuss the following questions with a partner, in small groups or in a large group with your teacher.

1. What was the "personality" of the company on your last job? In what ways (verbal or nonverbal) was this communicated to you?

2. Can you compare work behavior in your field in America and in your native country?

Putting It to Work: Communicating on the Job

In any situation where people must communicate with each other, misunderstandings can take place. It is important not only to listen carefully, but also to clarify any points that you have not understood.

Practice the following expressions, which can be used when you need clarification.

Could you repeat that once more, please?

I'm sorry, I didn't quite understand you.

I didn't catch what you want me to do.

Let me make sure I understood what you said. You want me to . . .

"Let Me Make Sure I Understood What You Said" is a listening exercise. Have your partner read to you one of the instruction paragraphs that follow. Then ask your partner questions about anything that isn't clear, such as dates and whether times are A.M. (morning) or P.M. (afternoon or evening). Take notes in order to recall the instructions later.

Example: Student A: Please call the airport and find out about flights to Chicago on Thursday the sixteenth. I want to leave before nine o'clock, and return Friday the seventeenth not later than six. Find out what airlines have flights at these times, and see if there is any difference in fares.

Student B: Let me repeat that. You want me to call the airport and find out about flights to Chicago on Thursday the sixteenth. You want to leave before nine o'clock. Is that nine o'clock in the morning?

Student A: Right, nine A.M.

Student B: And you want to return on Friday the seventeenth not later than six. You want a flight that leaves Chicago no later than six P.M., is that right?

Student A: Yes, six in the evening.

Student B: And you want me to find out which airlines have flights at those times and see if there is any difference in fares.

Student A: Right, you've got it!

1. Please call Mr. Frey and tell him I was delayed at my last appointment and I will be about half an hour late to the meeting. Please apologize and tell him I hope this will not inconvenience him.

2. I want you to make two copies of each of these two letters. File the originals and send the other two copies to Mrs. Sherman. Then xerox and collate one copy of this statistical report and send the xeroxed copy to Mr. Long.

3. Please contact Mr. Miller, Ms. Diamond and Ms. Robbins, and find out if they can make a meeting on Tuesday at ten to discuss the reorganization of testing procedures. If they can't come at that time, another possibility is Wednesday at two, but I prefer Tuesday because Wednesday afternoon is less convenient for me.

4. Get in touch with Bob Shoneman at Olympia Office Supply and tell him that they delivered four bulletin boards yesterday, but I ordered blackboards. I would like someone to come and pick up the bulletin boards and bring the blackboards as soon as possible . . . definitely before Thursday.

5. Because of the snowstorm, there will be no class next week, but the semester will be extended by one week. Therefore the last class will be May 22 instead of May 15. Also, on Friday we will follow Monday's schedule.

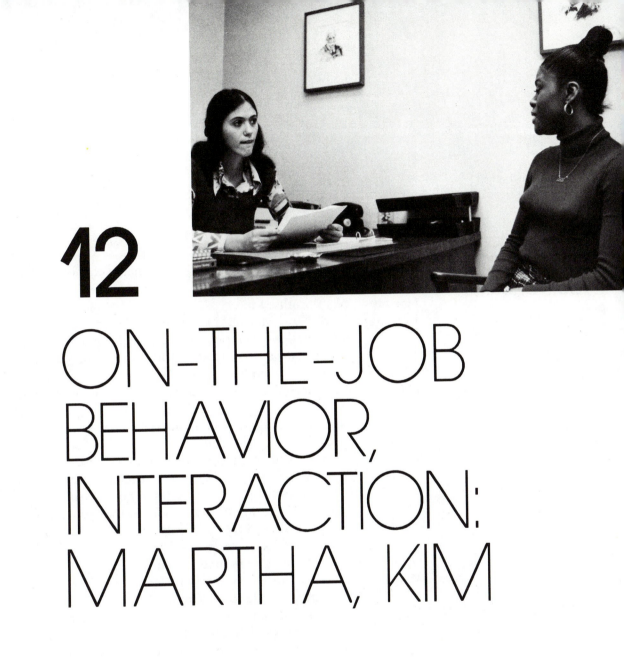

12

ON-THE-JOB
BEHAVIOR,
INTERACTION:
MARTHA, KIM

I. The Evaluation: Cost Effectiveness

Dorothy: Hello, Martha, come in. Have you had a chance to look over your evaluation?

Martha: Yes, Dorothy, I have.

Dorothy: Good. Now, Martha, I'd like to talk over some of the points in this evaluation. Of course, none of these things should come as a complete surprise to you, because I've mentioned them before.

Martha: Well, Dorothy, I don't understand why you wrote that my overall performance is not satisfactory. I come early, I do my work, and you know that I work very hard.

Dorothy: Of course you do, Martha, and I think you are an excellent worker. You never waste your time with things like personal calls or long lunches. The reason I have marked this rating unsatisfactory is that you are still not using your time effectively. You spend much too much time doing clerical tasks rather than tasks that are more directly related to your position.

Martha: That is because I want my work to be the best. I can't trust other people to do it properly.

Dorothy: I understand your feelings, but, for example, last week you spent a whole day working on your statistical report. I think you typed it over three times. Because of that, we were not able to start our new project. Other people have the responsibility for typing reports. Your knowledge and experience in this field are more valuable to the company than perfectly typed reports.

Martha: But suppose the typists spoil my work—it's a reflection on me.

178

Dorothy: Yes, but when you try to be a perfectionist, you end up using your time inefficiently, and it just isn't cost effective to the organization. You know, Martha, we really value you as an employee, and we want to see you spend more of your time doing what you were hired to do.

Martha: Yes, you are right. What can I do now?

Dorothy: I'm recommending an extension of six weeks to your probationary period. During those six weeks I want you to come in and talk over any problems you have in managing your work load.

Martha: Dorothy, I will. Thank you. (Martha was very upset about this, but she realized she had to rethink her approach to her work.)

II. The Evaluation: Communicating

"Come in, Kim. Have a seat, please," said Bill Williams, the manager. This was Kim's first experience with evaluations. After only six months he was due for a raise if this evaluation was satisfactory.

"Kim," began Bill Williams, "I am very pleased with the quality of your work. I have nothing but superlatives for your dedication and your hard work. My only concern is that you don't seem to take enough underline{initiative}."

"But," replied Kim, "I have always completed every assignment you have given me, Mr. Williams."

"I know that, Kim. And please, call me Bill. But what I expect is for you to think independently and take the initiative in introducing new ideas. I need more underline{input} from you—more underline{feedback} on how things are going. I don't need a "underline{yes man}." You never tell me what you think. You just smile as though everything is fine."

"But," said Kim, "I feel that since you are my superior, it would be underline{presumptuous} of me to tell you what to do."

"I'm not asking you to tell me what to do, but what you think we could do. To make suggestions. I hired you because I respect your experience in this field, but you are not communicating your thoughts to me."

"Yes, I see. I'm not accustomed to this, but I will try to do as you say . . . Bill."

"Good, then. I expect to hear more from you at staff meetings or at any other time you want to discuss an idea with me."

"Yes, of course. Thank you, Mr. Will . . . Bill."

What Happened?

Circle the letter of the word or words that best complete the statement.

1. Martha's rating was
   a. satisfactory.
   b. unsatisfactory.
   c. probation.

2. Martha's supervisor told her that she
   a. does her clerical work poorly.
   b. wastes time with personal calls.
   c. doesn't use her time effectively.

3. Martha agreed to change her way of working because
   a. she agreed with the supervisor.
   b. she had no choice.
   c. she wanted to save money for the organization.

4. Kim's employer feels that he
   a. doesn't give enough input.
   b. is not dedicated to the job.
   c. laughs too much (is too happy).

5. Kim's employer wants him to *take the initiative.* This means
   a. to offer ideas and suggestions before being asked.
   b. to offer ideas and suggestions after being asked.
   c. to take control of the department.

Hidden Meanings

Think about the following questions carefully before discussing in class. If necessary, refer to the story.

1. Why is Martha's inappropriate use of time costing her company money?

2. Why is insisting on perfection not the most efficient way to use time?

3. What must Martha learn to do?

4. Is Kim comfortable calling his boss by his first name? Why or why not?

5. Why do you think Kim usually "smiles as though everything is fine"?

Circle the letter of the expression that has the same meaning as the underlined word or words.

1. The supervisor recommended adding an <u>extension</u> to Martha's probationary period.
   a. evaluation
   b. end
   c. additional time

2. Kim's boss wanted more <u>feedback</u> from him.
   a. courtesy
   b. changes
   c. reactions

3. Martha's <u>rating</u> was not satisfactory.
   a. grade
   b. notice
   c. time

4. Every employee has to pass a <u>probationary period</u>.
   a. a written test
   b. a trial period before an evaluation
   c. a three-month period

5. He thought it would be <u>presumptuous</u> of him to tell his employer what to do.
   a. too friendly
   b. too arrogant or forward
   c. too knowledgeable

Complete each statement using one of the vocabulary words underlined in the text.

1. Your opinions, ideas, and suggestions are called your

_____ .

2. A judgment or rating of the effectiveness of your work is an

_____ .

3. Starting something on your own is called taking the

_____ .

4. Information about the results of your actions is called

_____ .

5. A person who wants to be perfect is a _____ .

6. A man who is always in agreement with what the boss says is a

_____ .

7. The work you are expected to finish is your

_____   _____ .

Understanding Words

Which statement is a good example of the meaning of the vocabulary word? Circle A or B.

1. recommend
   A. "If you are looking for a gift for your daughter, here is a book that she will probably like. We sell a lot of them to teenage girls."
   B. "If you are looking for a book for your daughter, the books for young people are in the rear of the store on the right-hand side."

2. presumptuous
   A. "Miss, I have been sitting in this restaurant for forty-five minutes, and nobody has taken my order. I think the service here is absolutely terrible."
   B. "Professor, I'm a student in your class, and I don't think you are teaching this subject correctly—I could teach it much better."

3. feedback
   A. "We sent a questionnaire to one hundred people who received our free sample, and fifty-two responded that they liked it very much and will buy it."
   B. "Please send these cans of cat food back to the factory. They are in poor condition."

4. input
   A. "Everyone at this meeting has given his or her opinion, and I would like to give mine. My opinion is that we should not go ahead with this project."
   B. "Excuse me, but I didn't hear what you said. What is the date of our next meeting?"

5. superlatives
   A. "I have no complaints about his work. It's fine."
   B. "She is one of the finest engineers in the business. Her technical skills are the best, and she is a most dedicated and hardworking employee."

Learning through Practice: Present Unreal Conditions

In this type of conditional statement, the past tense of the verb is used in the *if* clause, and *would, could,* or *might* is used in the answer clause. *To be* always takes the form of *were.*

> Example: If I *had* a million dollars, I *would* buy a co-op.

Note: A present unreal conditional always describes a situation which does not exist.

> Example: I am not the president of the United States, but if I *were* the president, I *would* help the poor.
>
> I don't know her number, but if I *knew* her number, I *would* call her.

Answer each question with a complete sentence.

1. If you were the mayor of this city, what would you do?

   _____

   _____

2. If you had a million dollars, what would you do?

   _____

   _____

3. If you were the president, what would you do about unemployment?

   _____

   _____

4. If you saw smoke coming out of a window, what could you do?

   _____

   _____

5. If you saw a robbery in the street, what would you do?

   _____

   _____

6. If you could not keep an appointment, what would you do?

   _____

   _____

7. If you could speak English perfectly, what would you do?

   _____

   _____

8. If you could travel anywhere in the world, where would you go?

   _____

   _____

9. If you were sick on a work day, what could you do?

   _____

   _____

10. If you had more time, what could you do?

   _____

   _____

Say It This Way

Match the idioms in Column A with the definitions in Column B.

Column A	Column B
a. to talk over	____general
b. to do over	____to start something on one's own
c. overall	____to discuss
d. to reflect on me	____to do again
e. to take initiative	____to show something about me

In many places of business there is some type of evaluation, or employee rating, following a probationary period. After that, there is usually a yearly evaluation, or *performance appraisal*. On the basis of the evaluation, the employee may be recommended for a promotion or a salary increase, or for termination of employment.

The supervisor usually discusses the evaluation with the employee and makes suggestions for improvement. The employee must read and sign the evaluation; it then goes into the employee's personnel file, which contains other relevant documents such as the employee's résumé and references.

A sample evaluation form is printed on the following pages. On this form, employees are rated according to the following scale:

    S = Satisfactory
    U = Unsatisfactory
    I = Not satisfactory now but showing improvement.

Other evaluation forms may use a number system or verbal ratings such as *outstanding, superior, good, fair,* and *poor*. This evaluation* is used for clerical employees. Review the form with your teacher. When you understand the various categories, imagine what the form would look like if it were your evaluation.

* Used and adapted courtesy of Federation Employment and Guidance Service, New York, NY.

EVALUATION FORM (CLERICAL)

	Supporting Data
I. *LEARNING ABILITY* 1. Comprehension: ability to **grasp** ideas and understand new methods and instructions ☐ 2. Memory: ability to remember facts, detailed instructions, methods and procedures ☐	Supporting Data
II. *KNOWLEDGE OF JOB* 1. General knowledge of company objectives and **set-up** of office in relation to own duties ☐ 2. Knowledge of own job: mastery of details involved in own work and duties; mastery of skill, dexterity, and techniques required in performance of job ☐	Supporting Data
III. *PRODUCTION OF WORK* 1. Rate of work: speed of accomplishment; rapidity as worker ☐ 2. Volume of work: **output** as compared with standard of group ☐ 3. Consistency: steadiness of production; **extent** to which employee maintains rate and volume of work with little supervision ☐	Supporting Data

IV. *QUALITY OF PERFORMANCE*
   1. Organization of work: extent to which employee is **systematic** and **methodical** in conduct of work □
   2. **Accuracy: reliability** and accuracy of work □
   3. **Neatness** and order: condition of work turned out; care of equipment □

Supporting Data

V. *RELATIONSHIP TO STAFF*
   1. Personal relations with staff members: ability to get along with associates, supervisors, and those working under her/him □
   2. Cooperativeness: ability to obtain cooperation from others; readiness to cooperate with others □

Supporting Data

VI. *WORKING UNDER SUPERVISION*
   1. **Compliance** with rules and regulations of office: ability to carry out instructions while regarding methods, policies, and procedures □
   2. **Flexibility:** positiveness of attitude with which assignments and responsibilities are **accepted,** degree of willingness and **graciousness** (or **resentment**) with which unwelcome assignments are carried out □

Supporting Data

3. Attitude toward criticism and suggestions: extent to which employee is **receptive** to comments, criticism, and suggestions; extent of improvement made as a result of criticism, suggestions, and instructions ☐	
VII. *ATTENTION AND INTEREST IN JOB*	Supporting Data
1. Conscientiousness: attendance and punctuality; **diligence** and **concentration** during work hours ☐	
2. Interest in further self-development: willingness to take on difficult tasks, assume extra responsibilities, and seek information to become more valuable to company ☐	
3. Initiative and originality: contribution to staff meetings; **constructive** suggestions to improve methods of operation and procedures in own job and in company ☐	
VIII. *PERSONAL FACTORS*	Supporting Data
1. Manner and **tact:** extent to which employee **conforms** to accepted rules of conduct ☐	
2. Appearance: neatness and appropriateness of dress ☐	

IX. *DEPENDABILITY AND JUDGMENT*

Supporting Data

1. Reliability: accuracy and **thoroughness** in completing tasks; consistency in following through; ability to plan realistically and not make promises that cannot be **fulfilled.** ☐
2. Use of judgment (common sense): ability to analyze situations and people; soundness of decisions ☐

X. *GENERAL OBSERVATION AND SUMMARY*

1. Data for personal guidance: List (a) strong and weak points; (b) any personal adjustments that may make employee more useful; (c) promotion possibilities, i.e., qualities that show executive or supervisory abilities and readiness to assume greater responsibilities or more difficult work.
2. Has this employee accomplished any unusually **meritorious** piece of work, or made an important contribution entitling him or her to special recognition? State details.
3. Has there been anything in the work, conduct, or attitude of this employee that deserves criticism?
4. Value to company in present job: give your overall estimate of this employee's service during the evaluation period.

EMPLOYEE _____

POSITION _____

RATED BY _____

SIGNED _____ DATE _____

Glossed Words

(to) **grasp**	(to) understand
set-up	the way in which anything is arranged or organized
output	the work produced
extent	degree
systematic	carried on in a step-by-step procedure
methodical	orderly
accuracy	correctness
reliability	dependability; trustworthiness
neatness	good order and clean
compliance	obeying
flexibility	adaptability
graciousness	courtesy
resentment	feelings of being treated unjustly
receptive	open
diligence	long, steady application to one's occupation
concentration	close attention to what what one is doing
constructive	helpful
tact	saying things in a way not to hurt others
(to) **conform**	(to) comply; act or be in agreement with
thoroughness	completeness
fulfilled	carried out
meritorious	deserving reward or praise

What's It All About?

Answer the following questions with your teacher or in writing on a separate sheet of paper

1. On the average, how often is an employee evaluated in an American company?

2. What can a good, or bad, evaluation do for an employee?

3. What happens to the written evaluation form after the evaluation is finished?

4. Can you match the terms in column A with the definitions in column B?

A	B
a. organized	____ diplomatic
b. accurate	____ systematic
c. neat	____ dependable
d. hard-working	____ understanding
e. tactful	____ orderly
f. punctual	____ correct
g. reliable	____ dexterity
h. consistent	____ steady
i. skill	____ on time
j. speed	____ diligent
k. comprehension	____ rapidity

Can We Talk?

Discuss the following question with a partner, in small groups, or in a large group with your teacher.

What kind of evaluation processes, if any, do employees go through in your native country?

Putting It to Work

You are the supervisor with the responsibility for evaluating the following people. What would you say to them? In a small group, discuss something positive and something negative to say in each case.

1. A job counselor who has to advise many people each week, but becomes very involved with each person and does not complete his required reports.

2. A secretary who makes many personal calls to her friends, but is an excellent typist and gets her work done on time.

3. A bookkeeper who is very accurate but who comes fifteen minutes late every morning because she has to drop off her child at school.

4. A mechanic who takes several hours to make a part that is needed because he thinks it will save money for his boss.

5. An employee who is very efficient, but on her own decides not to take her lunch hour, and to leave an hour earlier so she can avoid the rush hour.

6. An engineer who spends hours trying to solve minor problems that are very time consuming and impossible to solve.

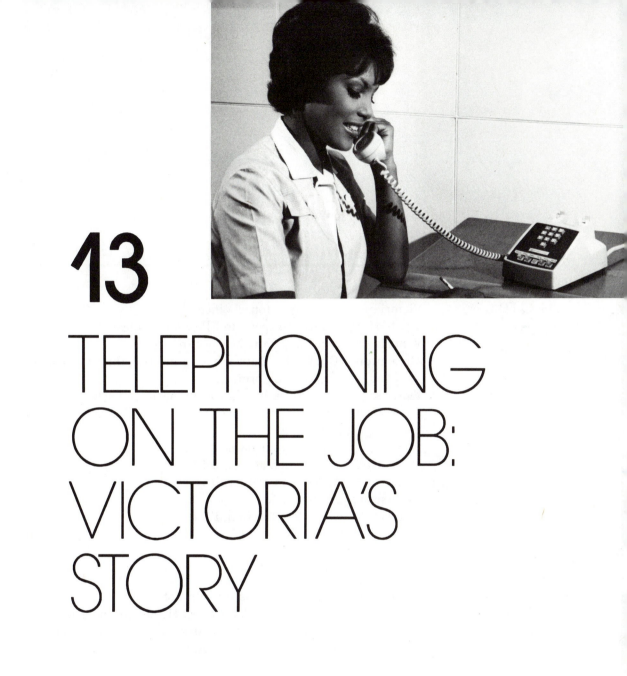

13
TELEPHONING ON THE JOB: VICTORIA'S STORY

Assumptions:
A 10:00 a.m.
Telephone
Conversation

Victoria: Hello, Ms. Jones' office.
Mr. Jenson: I'd like to speak to Ellen Jones, please.
Victoria: I'm sorry, but she's <u>not in</u>.
Mr. Jenson: Oh, really? But we have a meeting this afternoon on the housing project.
Victoria: Would you like to leave a message for her?
Mr. Jenson: Well . . . since she's not in, please have her call me tomorrow.
Victoria: What is your name, please?
Mr. Jenson: This is Bob Jenson calling.
Victoria: Where can she reach you?
Mr. Jenson: At my office.
Victoria: O.K., Mr. Johnson, I'll tell her.

One Hour Later

Ellen Jones: Victoria, who is this Mr. Johnson?
Victoria: I don't know, Ms. Jones. He called and I told him you weren't in. He said something about a meeting on the housing project.
Ellen Jones: A meeting? Johnson? And he wants me to call him tomorrow? What's his number?
Victoria: He said to call him at his office.
Ellen Jones: I don't know any Mr. Johnson. Didn't you ask him what company he was with?
Victoria: He didn't say.

194

Ellen Jones: Well, Victoria, that doesn't help me. I don't know who Mr. Johnson is, I don't know where he works, and I don't have a number where he can be reached. I'll just have to wait until he calls again.

Victoria: I'm sorry, Ms. Jones. He said, "Have her call me at the office," and I thought you had his telephone number.

Ellen: Hello, Bob? Have you forgotten our 2 o'clock meeting to discuss the projected increase in costs?

Bob: No, I didn't forget. I called you this morning and your secretary told me that you weren't in. I assumed our meeting was cancelled. I was surprised that you hadn't called me.

Ellen: But I've been here all day, in and out of meetings.

Bob: She didn't tell me that—she just said you weren't in today.

Ellen: Oh, dear. I'm sorry, but there's been a misunderstanding. I'll have to teach my new secretary how to take a message.

Answer the following questions.

1. When Mr. Jenson asked for Ellen Jones, what did Victoria answer?

   _____

2. What did Mr. Jenson assume?

   _____

3. When Mr. Jenson gave his name, did Victoria catch it correctly?

   _____

4. When Mr. Jenson said, "Have her call me at the office," what did Victoria assume?

   _____

5. What was Ellen Jones' response to the message Victoria gave her? What didn't she know?

_____

6. At 2:30 that day, what did Ellen Jones think?

_____

7. What did she do?

_____

8. What misunderstanding had taken place?

_____

9. Did Mr. Jenson repeat Victoria's words accurately to Miss Jones?

_____

Finding
the Definition

Circle the letter of the expression that has the same meaning as the underlined word or words.

1. He assumed that the meeting was <u>cancelled</u>.
   a. going to be held
   b. called off
   c. already finished.

2. Mr. Jenson <u>assumed</u> that Miss Jones was out of her office for the day.
   a. said
   b. knew
   c. supposed

3. They didn't have a meeting because of a <u>misunderstanding</u>.
   a. argument
   b. problem in communication
   c. cancellation

4. "I'm sorry, but Ms. Jones is <u>not in</u>."
   a. away from her desk
   b. out of the office for an indefinite period of time.
   c. sick at home

5. So many people were sick, we decided to <u>call off</u> the party.
   a. cancel
   b. have
   c. attend

*Each of the following statements is either an assumption, which is an
acceptance of something as true without proof, or a misunderstanding, which is a mistake in communication or comprehension. Read
each statement and then put* A, *for assumption, or* M, *for misunderstanding, in the blank space.*

_____ 1. "I thought you said the meeting was at 8:30 A.M. today, not
8:30 P.M."

_____ 2. "She didn't say she had any transportation problem, so I
suppose she has some way of getting to the party."

_____ 3. "Oh, I'm sure the students know their irregular verbs—
they are all at the intermediate level."

_____ 4. "I didn't hear from you, so I thought you were coming to
the party."

_____ 5. "I thought you said you were going away *for a month*."
"No, no, I said I was going to *Vermont*."

_____ 6. "I don't have an appointment, but if I go there and wait in
the office, the counselor will have to see me."

_____ 7. "Maria usually doesn't eat Chinese food, so I don't think
she wants to come with us."

_____ 8. "I'm really shocked. Last week Sally asked me if I wanted
a box of Girl Scout Cookies, and I said yes, and now I have
to pay five dollars for it."

_____ 9. "You said we would discuss it again today. I thought you
were going to call me."
"I thought *you* were going to call *me*."

_____10. "Just tell him John called, and ask him to call me back.
He knows my number."

Learning through Practice: Included Questions

Observe the word order when a noun clause is the *object* of the main verb. In this exercise, all noun clauses begin with question words.

Change each noun clause to a question.

1. I don't know who Mr. Johnson is.

   _____ QUESTION: Who is Mr. Johnson? _____

2. I don't know where he works.

   _____ QUESTION: Where does he work? _____

3. I didn't hear what you said.

   _____

4. I don't know who that man is.

   _____

5. I know what you mean.

   _____

6. I don't have a number where he can be reached.

   _____

Change each question to an included question.

1. When is she expected back?

   I'm not sure when she is expected back _____.

2. Where will next week's meeting be?

   I will let you know _____.

3. How long will the meeting last?

   I don't know exactly _____.

4. When will he be available for a conference?

   I will ask him _____.

5. Who is the sales representative in our area?

    Please hold on; I will find out _____ .

6. How long ago did he leave?

    Just a moment; I'll see if anyone here knows _____ .

Sometimes an included question is used because it sounds more polite than a direct question.

7. Who is calling?

    May I ask _____ .

8. What is this in reference to?

    May I tell her _____ .

Say It This Way

There are a number of pairs of words that are spelled alike but that are stressed on the first syllable when they are nouns or adjectives and on the second syllable when they are verbs.

    At pres'·ent, we have no openings.

    He will pre·sent' the idea to the board.

The stress does not change when an ending is added.

    The work is pro·gress'·ing nicely.

Some common words in this group are:

conduct	increase	produce
conflict	perfect	progress
contest	permit	project
contract	present	protest

Place a stress mark (') over the appropriate syllable in each of the words in heavy type, to show where the stress goes.

1. His **conduct** during the interview did not increase his chances of being hired.

199

2. He **protested** that he needed time to **perfect** his technique.

3. Have you made any **progress** with that new **project**?

4. The **contracts** will be **presented** to the clients at the meeting tomorrow.

5. We are **projecting** a large increase in sales next year.

6. The company does not **permit** its employees to accept any **presents** from people they do business with.

7. Do you plan to **contest** the charge that you have a **conflict** of interest?

8. Under the **present** laws, you must obtain a **permit** to sell **produce** in the street.

9. The firm is **conducting** a **contest** among its employees.

10. It is **perfectly** clear that your **conflicting** ideas will not **produce** the results we want.

Getting the Facts: Telephoning on the Job

When you are taking a message over the telephone, it is very important to get as much information as possible. Lack of information, incorrect assumptions, misspellings of names or places, and misunderstandings can cost a company time, money, and good will ("good will" is the caller's positive feeling about the company).

Here are some tips about answering the telephone on the job:

1. Answer with a pleasant greeting and a name (the name of the company, the department, your name, or the name of the person whose phone you are answering).
2. Write down the name of the caller and the company he or she is calling from. Repeat this information to the caller to make sure it is correct. Ask the caller to spell the names for you, and repeat the spelling to make sure you have written the information correctly.
3. Ask the caller for a number where he or she can be reached, and make sure it is clear whether he or she will call again or whether your employer or coworker should return the call.

4. Write down the date and time of the call, who the message is for, and your name or initials.

Answer the following questions with your teacher or in writing on a separate sheet of paper.

1. How do misunderstandings over the telephone affect the company?

2. What information must you get when taking a telephone message?

3. What should you do to make sure that your information is correct?

Discuss the following question with a partner, in small groups, or in a large group with your teacher.

Do you find speaking on the telephone difficult? Why?

Read the following dialogue with a partner. Use the message slip that follows the dialogue to take the message.

Receptionist: J. and G. Appliances; may I help you?
Caller: Yes. I need to speak to the manager, please.
Receptionist: He is not available at the moment. May I ask what this is in reference to?
Caller: I bought a dishwasher two months ago, and it isn't working well. I would like a refund or a new machine.
Receptionist: I see. Mr. Bronson won't be in his office until this afternoon, but I will leave a message for him. What is your name and phone number, sir?
Caller: Michael Carter, 347-1843.

Receptionist: Would you spell your name, please?
Caller: C-A-R-T-E-R
Receptionist: And would you repeat your number, please?
Caller: 347-1843.
Receptionist: That's 347-1843. When did you buy the dish-washer?
Caller: June third of this year.
Receptionist: And what is the brand or model number?
Caller: It's a Kensington Model thirty-eight B.
Receptionist: Fine. When Mr. Bronson returns I'll give him the information.
Caller: Oh, I'll be out for a couple of hours. Could you have him call me after three-thirty?
Receptionist: After three-thirty. Yes, I'll tell him. Thank you for calling, and sorry for the inconvenience.
Caller: Thank you. Goodbye.

WHILE YOU WERE OUT

To _____

Date _____ Time _____

Name _____

of _____

Phone _____

☐ telephoned	☐ please call
☐ returned your call	☐ will call again
☐ wants appointment	☐ urgent

Message _____

_____

_____

_____

_____

_____

Operator

Working in pairs, construct a dialogue for each of the following situations. Student A is the caller. Student B is the person being called.

1. Taking a Message

   Student A:

   Call the Burton Apartment Locating Bureau to find out if the apartment you just looked at is still available. Your agent's name is Mrs. Theodore. If Mrs. Theodore is not in, leave your name and number so that she can return the call as soon as possible. (You are very interested in the apartment.)

   Student B:

   You work for the Burton Apartment Locating Bureau. The Bureau has two agents and they are both out of the office. Since you cannot help the person who is calling, offer to take a message.

2. Leaving the Telephone

   Student A:

   Call the Second National Bank to ask for the balance in your checking account, number 0238656007. You cannot understand why a check you wrote for fifteen dollars has just "bounced" because you know you have more than that in your account.

   Student B:

   You work for the Second National Bank. A customer calls to ask for the balance in his checking account. Get the number of the checking account. Explain why you need to leave the telephone. When you return, tell the caller that his balance is $48.50. Explain to the caller that the check "bounced" because the money in the account was deposited by check, and it had not cleared as yet. It takes five working days for money deposited by check to clear.

3. Requesting Accurate Information

   Student A:

   You are the union representative for your department. You need to contact four employees who are out sick to inform them of an important meeting. One of the numbers you have just called is incorrect, and you got the wrong person. Call the personnel office of your company and verify the four telephone numbers that you have.

Amron, Harold	390-6248
Beaumarchais, Marie	443-9820
Boca, Marisa	251-5599
Turner, James	290-2575

Student B:

You work in the personnel office of a transportation company. The union representative for one of the departments is calling you. It will be necessary to leave the phone to get the necessary information. Give the telephone numbers clearly. These are the correct numbers.

Amron, Harold	390-6248
Beaumarchais, Marie	443-9820
Boca, Marisa	251-5589
Turner, James	290-2577

Useful Phrases to Help You Sound Good on the Telephone

1. *Answering the call:*
   R.E.O. Company, good morning.
   Mr. Romeo's office, may I help you?
   Order Department, _____ speaking.

2. *Taking messages:*
   Miss Jones has stepped away from her desk for a moment.
   I expect her back very shortly.
   She's in a meeting.
   She's not in at the moment.
   She's not in just now.
   She's out of the office at the moment.
   She has left for the day.

   May I have her call you?
   May I take a message?
   Would you like to leave a message?

3. *Asking for clarification:*

   I'm sorry, I didn't get the name (number).
   Would you repeat that number, please?
   Would you spell that for me, please?
   Did you say . . . ?
   Let me repeat to make sure I understand what you said.
   I want to be sure that I have this right.
   I'd like to be sure that I understand.
   That's . . . (repeat number or spelling).

4. *Leaving the phone:*

   Hold on just a moment, please.
   I have another call; will you hold on, please?
   Hold on; I'll be with you in a moment.
   Please hold on while I get that information.

   Thank you for waiting.

5. *Expressing regret:*

   I'm sorry you had that difficulty.
   I'm sorry to keep you waiting.
   We've been having trouble with our telephone all morning.

6. *Completing the conversation:*

   Thank you for calling, Mr. Smith.
   I'm glad I was able to help.
   You're welcome, Miss Raskin. Goodbye.

7. *Assuring the caller:*

   I'll tell her you called.
   I'll have him call you.
   I'll give her your message as soon as she gets back.
   I'll ask him to give you a call.
   I'll tell her you'll be here at nine-thirty tomorrow morning.

14

UPWARD MOBILITY: LISA'S STORY

Lisa sat staring at the clock thinking, "Can this be true? Have I really finished going to school?" She thought of how long she had actually been attending the Armstrong Business School. She couldn't believe that it was only eight months—two semesters! It had seemed twice as long.

Lisa had been in the United States for fifteen months. Back in her native country, she had been a bookkeeper, but when she arrived here, without any knowledge of English, she found it almost impossible even to get an interview. Now the placement counselor at the business school had set up two job interviews for her.

The first interview was for a job as an assistant bookkeeper for a small but well-known advertising agency. When she entered the building, Lisa was impressed by the spacious lobby and the clean, elegant construction of the building. Getting off the elevator at the tenth floor, she was delighted by the beauty of her surroundings, the shiny glass doors leading to the office, the carpets, and the gleaming desks. "What a beautiful place to work in," she thought.

Lisa was interviewed by the boss's son, who handled the financial side of the business. If she were hired, he would be her supervisor. The interview went very well. Lisa could tell that she was handling herself well and that the young man seemed favorably impressed with her. He asked her many questions, talked with her for an hour, and said he would be in touch with her after interviewing several other applicants.

The next day Lisa interviewed for another job as an assistant bookkeeper. This job was with a company in the garment district. The building was much older than the building that the advertising agency was in. The neighborhood was not very elegant, and seemed <u>dingy</u> and run down in comparison. However, it was a busy area and there was a doorman on duty in the building, so it seemed relatively safe. Lisa stepped into the old elevator and <u>prayed</u> that it would reach the fourth floor. It finally did, and she walked into the office of Mitchell Winterwear. She noticed that the floors were not carpeted, and the furniture looked old and <u>worn</u>. Everybody seemed <u>cramped</u> into small <u>cubicles</u>.

Lisa was interviewed by the personnel manager, a Mr. Smith, who explained the responsibilities of the assistant bookkeeper. This job paid a little more than the one at the advertising agency, and there was an excellent opportunity to move up. The present bookkeeper was an older woman who would be <u>retiring</u> soon. The new person would be in training for her position. This meant that before the year was up there would be a promotion and a <u>substantial</u> salary increase.

Mr. Smith then asked Lisa more specific questions about her skills and experience. He told her that he was very impressed with her qualifications, and that she was one of three people that he was considering for the job. Lisa smiled and politely thanked him, but she hardly heard what he was saying. In her mind she was back at the advertising agency in that beautiful office building where she knew she would be working. It was comfortable, it was a job she could handle, and it paid enough to live on.

What Happened?

Circle the letter of the word or words that best complete the statement.

1. Lisa had attended business school for
   a. one semester.
   b. eight months.
   c. fifteen months.

2. What Lisa liked about the job at the advertising agency was
   a. the elegant surroundings.
   b. the salary.
   c. the boss's son.

3. Lisa
   a. made a favorable impression on both interviewers.
   b. didn't do well on either interview.
   c. made a better impression in the first interview.

4. The bookkeeper at Mitchell Winterwear would retire soon because
   a. she was an older person.
   b. she didn't like the cramped office space.
   c. she was afraid of the elevator.

5. Lisa wasn't paying attention to the second interviewer because
   a. she was impolite.
   b. she didn't like Mr. Mitchell.
   c. she had decided that she wanted the first job.

Hidden Meanings

Think about the following questions carefully before discussing in class. If necessary, refer to the story.

1. Is Lisa ambitious (concerned with moving up the "career ladder")?

2. Do you think Lisa has long term or short term goals? Give a reason for your choice.

3. Why did Lisa pray that the elevator in the building of Mitchell Winterwear would reach the fourth floor?

4. What kinds of goals would each job help Lisa meet?

Finding the Definition

Circle the letter of the expression that has the same meaning as the underlined word or words.

1. She was uncomfortable because he was staring at her.
   a. looking steadily
   b. shouting
   c. waving

2. Lisa was <u>delighted</u> with the beautiful office building.
   a. surprised
   b. thankful
   c. highly pleased

3. The furniture looked old and <u>worn</u>.
   a. repainted
   b. used
   c. torn

4. A Cadillac is very <u>spacious</u> inside.
   a. elegant
   b. expensive
   c. roomy

5. Everyone was <u>cramped into small cubicles</u>.
   a. crowded into small compartments
   b. divided into small compartments
   c. assigned to small compartments

Finding the Word

Complete each statement using one of the vocabulary words under-lined in the text.

1. To speak to God is to _____ .

2. The environment around you is called your _____
_____ .

3. <u>Gleaming</u> is the same as _____ .

4. To stop working when you are older and live on a pension is to
_____ .

5. A compartment with walls but without a ceiling is a
_____ .

Understanding Words

Which statement is a good example of the meaning of the vocabulary word? Circle A or B.

1. stare
   A. That man has been looking at me for ten minutes.
   B. That man is beginning to speak.

2. pray
   A. I hope you and your family are in good health.
   B. Thank you, Lord, for our blessings, and we hope for good health and happiness in the coming days.

3. delighted
   A. It was nice meeting you.
   B. I am so happy to see you!

4. cramped
   A. I'm so tall that I have no room for my legs in the back seat of the car.
   B. There is room for all of us in the back of the car.

5. spacious
   A. There is plenty of room for everything in this apartment.
   B. We are spending a lot of money on exploring outer space.

6. shiny
   A. That floor is certainly clean.
   B. You can see your face reflected in that tabletop.

Learning through Practice: Comparative Form

Adjectives of one syllable form the comparative by adding *-er*. Some short adjectives double the final consonant before adding *-er*.

long	*longer*	big	big*ger*

Two-syllable adjectives ending in *y* also add *-er*. The *y* changes to *i* before the *-er*.

happy	happ*ier*	busy	bus*ier*

Other adjectives show the comparative with the word *more*.

beautiful   *more* beautiful   crowded   *more* crowded

A few adjectives have irregular comparative forms.

good   *better*   bad   *worse*

Fill in each blank with the comparative form of the adjective below it.

1. Of the two jobs, the one at Mitchell Winterwear offers a

   _____ opportunity for promotion.
         (favorable)

2. The garment district is a _____ neighbor-
                                    (noisy)

   hood. The advertising agency is in a _____
                                              (fashionable)

   neighborhood.

3. The advertising agency is _____ to trans-
                                   (convenient)

   portation than Mitchell.

4. The job at Mitchell pays a _____ salary
                                     (high)

   than the one at the advertising agency.

5. The surroundings at the advertising agency are certainly

   _____ and _____ .
         (elegant)   (spacious)

6. Mitchell Winterwear has much _____ of-
                                         (dingy)

   fices.

7. But the employees at the advertising agency didn't seem any

   _____ than those at Mitchell.
         (happy)

8. The employees at the advertising agency get a

   _____ vacation, but Mitchell has a
         (long)

   _____ benefits package.
         (good)

213

9. If I take the job at the advertising agency, I'll have to buy

_____ clothes; at Mitchell, the dress seems
        (expensive)

_____ .
        (informal)

10. I don't know when I've made a _____ de-
                                          (difficult)
cision.

Say It This Way

Match the idioms in Column A with the definitions in Column B.

Column A	Column B
a. to be in touch	____ in poor condition
b. in training for	____ to advance
c. the year was up	____ double the amount of time
d. run down	____ to keep in contact
e. twice as long	____ learning
f. to move up	____ the year ended

Getting the Facts: Upward Mobility

Pursuing a dream or goal in life requires a lot of work. For a newcomer, the dream of setting up a better life in a new country takes tremendous physical and emotional energy. After settling everyone in, finding employment, enrolling children (if any) in school, and establishing him- or herself socially, the newcomer has taken care of all the immediate needs. The newcomer's life begins to fall into a certain pattern. He or she may now have a fairly good understanding of the language, may have built up some security on the job, and may feel that the family is happy. This is the point at which some newcomers experience an **unsettling** feeling. The individual may begin to ask, "Where do I want to go from here? Am I willing to remain in this neighborhood where most people speak my native language, do the same things, live the same kind of life—or do I want a bigger apartment, a better car, more household comforts? How can I do this? How can I make more money?

What do I need to do? Should I learn more English? Should I learn another trade with which I can make more money in the future and get all the things I want?"

At this **stage**, the individual has to make a decision either to settle into the neighborhood he or she first **embraced**, **surrounded** by familiar faces, foods, and customs, or to reach for a different kind of life. To make this decision the individual needs to rethink how he or she looks at life and work.

There is a belief, often true, that upward **mobility** in America is the result of **perserverance**, hard work, initiative, and the desire to constantly improve one's position in life. The language is full of phrases like *going places, on the way up, rising to the top, on the right track, where are you heading?, and the ladder of success;* all refer to an individual's professional and financial advancement.

The desire to be upwardly mobile requires a re-examination of one's job skills. Moving upward means more than making a living on a day-to-day basis. It means looking into the future and planning how far you want to go, and what you need to do in order to get there. It means more time and effort on the job as well as adapting to the fast **rhythm** of the American way of life. It requires planning a **career**, not just finding a job or **making ends meet**.

The following story gives two perspectives on life and work.

Under the Olive Tree
(Two Philosophies)

A bus full of tourists passed by a grove of olive trees in _____. The bus stopped for repairs, and the tourists got off in order to stretch their legs. One of the tourists began to watch a young man who was sleeping under an olive tree. Slowly, the young man got up. He shook the olive tree and many olives fell on the ground. Then the young man picked them up and put them into a sack. He continued to shake the tree and pick up olives for half an hour. Then he stretched out again under the tree and rested.

"Excuse me," said the tourist. (He spoke a little of the native language.) "What are you going to do with those olives?"

"I'm going to take them to the market and sell them," answered the young man.

"And how much money will you get for them?" asked the tourist.

"Enough to live for a day," answered the young man.

"Then, why don't you shake the tree again, and get some more olives?" asked the tourist.

"Why?" asked the young man. "Why should I do that?"

The tourist answered, "If you pick olives for five or six hours, you will make more money."

"Why should I make more money?" asked the young man.

"If you make more money, you can buy a donkey and cart."

"And then what?" asked the young man.

"Then you can bring more olives to market."

"And then what?" asked the young man.

"When you make a lot of money, you can hire a man to work for you."

"And then what?" asked the young man.

"Then you will make much more money. You can buy a truck, and hire two or three men to work for you."

"And then what?" asked the young man.

"When you have enough money, you can build a factory and hire fifty men to work for you. You'll be a rich man!"

"And then what?" asked the young man.

"When you're a rich man, you won't have to work! You can sit and sleep under the olive trees all day if you want to!"

"Excuse me," said the young man, "but that's what I'm doing now."

And he stretched out and went back to sleep.

Glossed Words

unsettling	disturbing
stage	step or point in some process
(to) **embrace**	(to) accept eagerly
(to) **surround**	(to) encircle on all sides
upward mobility	movement to a higher economic or social status

perseverance	act of continuing or of not giving up even if difficult
rhythm	movement with a regular order of strong and weak elements
career	course of professional life or employment
(to) **make ends meet**	(to) keep one's expenses within one's income

What's It All About?

Answer the following questions with your teacher or in writing on a separate sheet of paper.

1. What are three expressions in English that show the American "upward" orientation?

2. What is a *career*? How is it different from a *job*?

3. What is meant by *the ladder of success*?

4. What decisions must a newcomer make once the basic needs are satisfied?

5. What must an individual re-examine if he or she buys into the concept of upward mobility?

Can We Talk?

Discuss the following questions with a partner, in small groups, or in a large group with your teacher.

1. What do you think of each philosophy in the story, "Under the Olive Tree?"

2. How has the concept of upward mobility affected your life?

3. How would you put off immediately answering an interviewer if a job is offered to you?

4. Is it necessary to jump at the first two job offers? How could you gain time to go on other interviews?

217

5. Why is upward mobility difficult for women in general, and for foreign women in particular?

Putting It to Work

Form small groups and decide which job you would advise Lisa to take. The group must reach a consensus (agreement). Each group should choose a reporter to tell the class of the group's decision. Consider the following questions.

1. What should Lisa take into consideration before making a decision?

2. What would you advise her to do?

3. How would you convince her to take the job you think is best?

4. What are the advantages of taking the first job?

5. What are the advantages of taking the second job?

15

RIGHTS AND FRINGE BENEFITS: LEE'S STORY

Lee sat at her desk in the small office, too tired to move. The clock said 6:45 P.M., and the office was almost empty. Evelyn, the other bookkeeper, was getting ready to leave the office. Lee sighed. She just couldn't understand how Evelyn had arranged to work just so much overtime and no more.

On her way out, Evelyn passed by Lee's desk. "You're really working late tonight, Lee," said Evelyn as she put on her coat. "You work overtime a lot, don't you?"

"Unfortunately, I do," replied Lee.

"You mean, you don't want to work overtime?" Evelyn asked.

For the first time, Lee began to talk about her problem. "At first I didn't mind," she told Evelyn. "Mr. Ames asked me to stay late and finish some work, and I was glad to do it. I was happy to make the extra money. But then he asked me to stay almost every evening. And recently he has asked me to work on some Saturdays, too. I don't know what to do. I need this job."

Evelyn took off her coat and sat down next to Lee. "You know, sometimes you have to negotiate your own working conditions. You have to decide exactly how much overtime you are able to put in, and then discuss with Mr. Ames what your needs are."

Lee's heart sank. She just hated to rock the boat. Things were going so well for her. She had finally landed this full-time job. She hated the thought of going in to Mr. Ames and confronting him with her problem. Besides, Mr. Ames, the boss, was a person of authority and she wasn't comfortable asking for changes. Wouldn't that be challenging his authority?

"Look," Evelyn said, "I'm sure that if you just go in and discuss this with Mr. Ames you will come up with a compromise.

Maybe he is under the impression that you want to work over-time."

After Evelyn left, Lee began to understand what she was saying. Lee thought back to the first interview she had with Mr. Ames. Everything had seemed very clear and up front back then.

Mr. Ames: Well, Miss Ross tells me that your bookkeeping skills are top-notch.
Lee: Thank you. That was very kind of her.
Mr. Ames: Yes; I need people like you, with brains and maturity. The job is yours if you want it.
Lee: Yes, I do. Thank you.
Mr. Ames: Good. Now, about the salary . . . are you aware that the salary is $13,000?
Lee: Yes.
Mr. Ames: Is that satisfactory?
Lee: Yes, it is.
Mr. Ames: And the hours are nine to five with one hour for lunch.
Lee: Yes, I understand. Miss Ross explained that to me.
Mr. Ames: Of course, there will be some overtime.
Lee: Well, that will be all right.
Mr. Ames: Especially during our busy season.
Lee: I understand.
Mr. Ames: (looking at his watch) Well, I'm pleased that you will be working with us. Will you be able to start next Monday?
Lee: Yes, that will be no problem.
Mr. Ames: (standing up and extending his hand) Excellent. Welcome aboard!
Lee: Thank you very much.

Lee remembered how excited and relieved she had been when she got this job. But it was very clear to her now, that what Mr. Ames had meant by "some overtime" was not what she had understood. One way or another, she had to resolve this problem. How could she do it? In her eagerness to get the job she hardly heard what he had said after "You've got the job if you want it." She should have asked for more specific information regarding the amount of overtime.

What Happened?

Circle the letter of the word or words which best completes the statement.

1. At first, Lee
   a. was happy to work overtime.
   b. minded working overtime.
   c. disliked working overtime.

2. Evelyn advised Lee to
   a. join the union.
   b. let the problem resolve itself.
   c. negotiate working conditions for herself.

3. In Lee's initial interview with Mr. Ames she did not clarify
   a. what her hours would be.
   b. how much overtime there would be.
   c. what her salary would be.

4. Evelyn felt that a discussion with the employer would result in a
   a. problem.
   b. challenge.
   c. compromise.

Hidden Meanings

Think about the following questions carefully before discussing in class. If necessary, refer to the story.

1. Why couldn't Lee understand how Evelyn had arranged to work just so much time and no more?

2. Why couldn't Evelyn understand why Lee was working overtime if she didn't want to?

3. What did Evelyn mean when she said ". . . discuss with Mr. Ames what your needs are?"

4. What was the misunderstanding about overtime at the initial interview between Lee and Mr. Ames?

5. Why did Lee feel uncomfortable about talking with Mr. Ames?

Circle the letter of the expression that has the same meaning as the underlined word or words.

1. Are you aware of the salary?
   a. Do you know . . .
   b. Are you satisfied with . . .
   c. Are you unhappy about . . .

2. We have to negotiate a new contract.
   a. get
   b. discuss
   c. ask for

3. After a great deal of discussion, we reached a compromise.
   a. an agreement that is acceptable to both sides
   b. a victory for both sides
   c. a defeat for one side

4. Her boss was a person of authority.
   a. wealth
   b. power
   c. maturity

Complete each statement using one of the vocabulary words underlined in the text.

1. To have a worry taken from your mind is to be

   _____ .

2. An obstacle, or something difficult to overcome, is a

   _____ .

3. A person in charge is a person in _____ .

4. If you face a problem directly, you are _____

   _____ it.

Understanding Words

Which statement is a good example of the meaning of the vocabulary word? Circle A or B.

1. negotiate
   A. "We want to discuss the union demands because we feel a 10 percent increase is not realistic."
   B. "We demand a salary increase."

2. relieved
   A. "Thank goodness you have come home safely. The weather is so dangerous for driving."
   B. "Thank you so much for driving me home. I really appreciate it."

3. compromise
   A. "We will accept this agreement only if you meet all our demands."
   B. "We will agree to an 8 percent increase if you agree to keep the number of sick days at its present level."

4. challenge
   A. "This course looks very difficult, but I want to try it—I'm sure I can do the work."
   B. "This course is too easy for me—I'm bored most of the time."

5. confront
   A. "I'd like to discuss a problem with you as soon as you have a moment."
   B. "I want to talk to you, but if you're busy now, it can wait."

Learning through Practice: Should, Should Have and Past Participle

Should indicates obligation. It is different from *must*, which conveys *necessity*.

Study these sentences:

We must eat in order to live.
We should eat nutritious food.
We mustn't eat poison.

We shouldn't smoke.

We must pay taxes.

We should take aspirin to relieve headaches.

The past tense of *should* is formed by adding *have* plus the *past participle.*

The car door was unlocked, and someone stole my radio.

I should have locked the car door.

Read each statement and then write what the person should have done.

Example: Lee didn't clarify what Mr. Ames meant by overtime. (ask how much overtime there was.)

Lee should have asked Mr. Ames how much overtime there was.

1. Victor didn't understand the necessity for appointments. (make an appointment.)

   _____

   _____

2. Martha left her job without giving notice. (give notice)

   _____

   _____

3. Marisa didn't want to consult the reference books in the library. (go to the library)

   _____

   _____

4. Joseph didn't give his qualifications for the personnel job. (tell Mrs. Mitchell why he was qualified for the job)

   _____

   _____

5. Peter didn't address his cover letter to a specific person. (find out who to send the letter to)

_____

_____

6. Gisela selected the wrong chair. (take the chair at the side of the desk)

_____

_____

7. Samuel was wrong to discuss his personal problems with the interviewer. (not speak about his personal problems)

_____

_____

8. Martha typed all her reports herself. (give them to the secretary)

_____

_____

9. Horace stayed too long on his vacation. (call the company)

_____

_____

Say It This Way

From the list below, choose an idiom that has the same meaning as the underlined phrase, and rewrite the complete sentence.

just so much
to mind
to rock the boat
to land a job
top notch
welcome aboard
her heart sank
to go to bat for someone (a baseball term)

1. That company is <u>first class</u> in the field of educational toys.

   _____

   _____

2. I don't <u>object to</u> working overtime.

   _____

   _____

3. The administration wanted to fire him, but the union <u>supported him</u> and he kept his job.

   _____

   _____

4. I can stand <u>only a certain amount of</u> rock and roll music, and that's all.

   _____

   _____

5. When she saw the long application form <u>she felt very discouraged</u>.

   _____

   _____

6. It was his first job in America, and he didn't want to <u>create difficulties</u>.

   _____

   _____

7. After Mr. Ames had hired Lee, he said "<u>Welcome to our company</u>."

   _____

   _____

8. She was relieved finally <u>to get some work</u>.

   _____

   _____

Getting the Facts: An Employee's Rights and Fringe Benefits

Every job has **fringe benefits**, some more than others. During the interviewing process a candidate needs to find out what those benefits are. Many times employers will offer a lower salary and increase the benefits to make a job more attractive; benefits can amount to 15 percent or more above the salary that is quoted. In this section we will talk about benefits and also about an employee's legal rights and about unions.

Company benefits

Insurance   Types of insurance include Blue Cross/Blue Shield, major medical, dental plan, prescription plan, and life insurance.

Leave   Types of leave include paid vacation days, holidays, sick days, and personal and religious days.

Disability retirement   Retirement with partial pay due to illness or injury that prevents the employee from working.

Pension   The money a person receives each month when he or she retires.

Tuition aid   Money that some companies will pay for courses that upgrade the employee's skills and improve performance; this is also called *tuition reimbursement*.

Company policies regarding salary increases and working conditions

Probationary period   A trial period during which the employee's performance is judged. If not satisfactory, the employee may be fired without other cause.

Increment   An increase in salary, usually automatic.

Cost-of-living increase   A raise in salary based on some official table of cost-of-living **fluctuation**, given **voluntarily** or **guaranteed** in the union contract.

Merit increase   A raise in salary based on job performance.

Promotion	Moving up from a lower level of responsibility and pay to a higher one, usually on the basis of performance. One reason an employee is supervised and evaluated is to assess promotability.
Seniority	Many places of employment where there is more than one employee have a seniority program. This means that the employees who have been with the company for a long time may have higher salaries, first choice for vacations, or protection when cuts in staff are considered.
Compensatory time	In some companies that do not pay for hours worked overtime employees can take off regular working hours to make up the time.

Legal rights and procedures

Employee safety	If you have any questions about the safety of your job regarding construction of buildings, equipment, and machinery, fire safety, or other health hazards, you may call the Department of Labor, Occupational Safety and Health Administration, or your state department of health.
Maximum hours	Beyond forty hours a week, employers **covered** by the Federal Wage, Hour, and Public Contracts Laws are required to pay certain employees time and a half, or overtime.
Minimum wage	The least amount of money that an employer in most industries can legally pay an employee.
Payroll deductions	From the monthly or weekly pay, there are **deductions** for social security coverage and federal, state and, local taxes. Social security coverage, also called Federal or F.I.C.A., is paid by both employer and employee. Deductions may also include health plan fees, savings, pension, contributions, and union dues.

Right to wages	If the employer does not pay for work that you have done, you have a right to sue. However, if the employee is in debt, a court may tell the employer to pay the employee's wage to the person or group to whom the employee owes money: this is called a *garnishment*.
Social security	A federal program to give **eligible** people an income when they retire. Every employee must have a social security number. People who are paid in cash are also supposed to pay for social security insurance.
Unemployment insurance	The money you get from the state while you are unemployed and looking for a job, if you meet the eligibility requirements. A person who was fired for **negligence** or who quit the job is not eligible.
Worker's compensation	In many states, if an employee is hurt on the job, *worker's compensation* can pay for medical bills. The supervisor should be notified immediately of any injury and should fill out a form for the State Industrial Accident Board. By law, information about worker's compensation should be posted where all employees can see it.
Equal opportunity employment	Any employer with more than fifteen employees cannot discriminate against an applicant because of color, sex, religion, or place of birth. If you feel you did not get a job because of discrimination, you can report it to Office of Federal Contract Compliance, U.S. Department of Labor, Washington D.C. 20210, or to the local division of the Department of Labor, which is under United States Government in your local telephone book.
Unions	A labor union is a group of employees who organize to get higher pay and better working conditions. Unions began in the years before laws protecting employees' rights had been passed.

230

In many fields, trades, or companies all personnel may be organized in a specific union. In such cases it may be obligatory to join that union to be on the same basis as other employees in that company.

Union representatives sit down with employers and try to work out problems; this is called *collective bargaining*. When union representatives and employers agree on a contract, the contract must be voted on and accepted by a majority of the union members. The contract then becomes a legal document that must be observed by both sides.

Membership in a union means being loyal to the union contracts and paying dues. In return, the union is supposed to protect the members' pay, working conditions, holidays, and vacation time, and to counsel and protect members with specific **grievances**.

In cases where union membership is optional, you must consider the advantages and disadvantages of belonging or not belonging.

Glossed Words

fringe benefits	all benefits an employee receives on the job
fluctuation	change
voluntarily	by one's own choice
guaranteed	promised; state with certainty
covered	included under
salary deductions	money taken from salary
eligible	qualified
negligence	carelessness
grievances	complaints

What's It All About

Match the terms in Column A with the definitions in Column B.

Column A

a. increment
b. promotion
c. tuition reimbursement
d. garnishment
e. probation
f. social security
g. pension

h. collective bargaining
i. grievance

j. compensation

Column B

____trial period
____F.I.C.A.
____complaint
____paying back
____salary increase
____advancement
____financial help for education
____retirement money
____court order to take employee's salary to pay debts
____negotiations between union and management

Can We Talk?

Discuss the following questions with a partner, in small groups or in a large group with your teacher.

1. What benefits does your employer offer?

2. Is there an overtime policy where you work? What is it?

3. What should Lee have asked Mr. Ames during the first interview?

4. Is there a union where you work? Does the union require employees to join?

5. In your native country, is it possible for two people doing the same job to be earning a different salary? If so, explain.

*Read the following interview, keeping in mind the concepts that you
have studied in this book.*

Secretary:	There is a Mr. Gomez to see you. Shall I send him in?
James:	On yes, send him in, please.
John:	(walks through the reception area to Mr. Johnson's office) Good morning, Mr. Johnson. I'm John Gomez.
James:	How do you do? Please have a seat and make yourself comfortable while I pull out your résumé, and . . . please call me James.
John:	(looks around for a comfortable chair and selects a spot) Would you mind very much if I pulled this chair up to the side of your desk?
James:	Not at all. Go right ahead. Now, let me just refresh my memory . . . may I call you John?
John:	Yes, of course.
James:	One of the reasons I asked you to come in for an interview is because of your experience abroad. We are expanding our company offices to Europe, and we will be needing people to work as intermediaries or liaisons in the U.S. We will need someone who understands both languages to review the reports, correspondence, and whatever else comes in from the European offices. I would like you to give me a little more detail about your experience, both in your native country and the United States.
John:	Of course. Before I start, can you give me more information about the position?
James:	Certainly. What would you like to know?
John:	What are the duties of the position?
James:	The title of the position is foreign liaison. You would be reviewing the reports that come in from one of the European branches, summarizing the information, and turning it over to the secretaries to type for the manager to review. There would be times when the information received is not clear, which means you'd contact the European offices to update the information. Many times you would be calling information in

233

	to them, making sure that the work is being submitted accurately, and so forth.
John:	It seems that it is very important to know the technical side of this job as well as the second language.
James:	Absolutely.
John:	I have a clearer picture of the position now and can see where my experience fits in. I speak my native language fluently, and am always taking courses to improve my second language, which is English. I have three years of experience working with computers back in my native country, so I'm familiar with all types of computers and printouts. I have extensive experience working with people from different parts of the world and at all levels. This is a field that I have been trained in and have successfully worked in for the past seven years. I'm looking for a position where I can grow professionally and financially. But most importantly, I am looking for a company where I can make a contribution.
James:	Let me ask you a question John, where do you see yourself in five years?
John:	I see myself constantly improving my skills and moving up in whatever company I join. Who would I be reporting to, James?
James:	You would be reporting directly to the first-line supervisor. This is an entry-level position, so you can really go as far as your abilities will take you or as far as you want to go. You seem to have the qualifications that we need for this job . . . . Tell me, John, how would you describe your personality?
John:	I am energetic and outgoing. I like to have something to do all the time. I sometimes push myself too hard when I get involved in my work. Also, I like to get a sense of completion when I'm on a project.
James:	We could use some of that energy.
John:	I would very much like the opportunity to work for your company. The position you described sounds like something that I could really get involved in and do well. What are the salary and benefits for this position?

James:	The starting salary is $17,000 with a performance review after three months and another review after six months with a consideration for an increment of up to 12 percent. After that, you would be reviewed every year, like everyone else, and at that time be considered for additional increments.
John:	What benefits does the company offer?
James:	In addition to the $17,000 salary, the benefits include Blue Cross/Blue Shield health insurance coverage, dental coverage, one sick day a month as well as one week of vacation after the first six months and two weeks after one year.
John:	I am very interested in the position. Would you be able to tell me where I stand in relation to the other applicants for this position?
James:	Well, I'm just about finished with the initial interviewing of all the applicants for this job, so I'll be narrowing it down to three by tomorrow. I will then ask those three to come back for a follow-up interview with the manager of the data processing department. I consider you a very strong possibility, John. I will be calling you to let you know for sure some time tomorrow. Will I be able to reach you at the number that is on your résumé?
John:	Yes. If I'm not in, you can leave a message with the receptionist and I'll call you back as soon as possible.
James:	Fine, John. You sound like the kind of person we can use around here. I look forward to the possibility of working with you.
John:	Likewise, James. I hope to hear some good news from you real soon. Thank you for your time. Have a good day! Bye now.
James:	Same to you. So long.

Analyzing
the Interview

1. What do you think are some of the good questions that John asked James?

2. What do you think are some of the bad questions that John asked James?

3. When James asked John to give "more details about his experience," how did John's answer give him an advantage?

4. Was John a good listener? How do you know?